THE
ANXIETY
GETAWAY

THE ANXIETY GETAWAY

How to Outsmart Your Brain's False Fear Messages and Claim Your Calm Using CBT Techniques

TURNER
PUBLISHING COMPANY

Turner Publishing Company
Nashville, Tennessee
www.turnerpublishing.com

Cover and Interior Design: Jermaine Lau

The Anxiety Getaway: How to Outsmart Your Brain's False Fear Messages and Claim Your Calm Using CBT Techniques

LCCN: 2020933912

ISBNs: (p) 978-1-64250-057-8 (e) 978-1-64250-058-5

BIBSAC: SEL036000—SELF-HELP / Anxieties & Phobias

Printed in the United States of America

AUTHOR'S NOTE

The patients described in this book are composites of patients I've had during the course of over twenty years in practice. They do not address individuals. In my work and the work of all psychologists, confidentiality is paramount. Therefore, I've taken careful steps to ensure patient privacy, such as providing fictitious names and removing any other identifiable features. All patient cases have either been combined or altered to protect privacy. Any resemblance to any actual person is entirely coincidental.

TABLE OF CONTENTS

INTRODUCTION

Welcome to the first step toward your anxiety getaway! The fact that you're reading this suggests you'd like to overcome the difficult, limiting, uncomfortable, and sometimes downright terrifying experience you call *anxiety*.

But are you sick and tired of it? I hope so. Why do I ask? Because that emotional state is a good catalyst for great change! How do you know if you're both "sick" *and* "tired" of anxiety? Well, you sort of know it when you feel it. But rather than risk being vague, I've got an easy test for you to determine if you're there. If you answer "yes" to at least three of the questions below, you will be crowned as "sick and tired of anxiety." Here it goes:

1. Do you dislike that your anxiety disrupts or interferes with your life?

2. Are you annoyed that anxiety inhibits you in some way?

3. Do you miss a time in the past when you didn't struggle with your current symptoms?

4. Do you feel like anxiety is your unwelcome companion, accompanying you to places or situations where it doesn't belong?

5. Do you envy those you believe do not "have anxiety"?

6. Do you dislike that you sometimes feel ashamed or embarrassed by your anxiety symptoms?

7. Are you troubled by a belief that anxiety reflects who you are?

8. Are you upset by the belief that people might see you as weak or incapable in some way?

9. Do you sometimes see yourself as weak or incapable for struggling with anxiety?

Answering "yes" to just three of these items means that you're ready to take on what's in these pages in order to claim your calm!

Now, this may or may not come as a surprise, but when you read on, you'll soon learn you can't defeat anxiety without... your lucky t-shirt. Wait! Scratch that. I meant without facing fear, of course. Hence, the subject of fear runs through the veins of this book (I was going to say arteries, but that didn't have the intensity I was looking for). To overcome your anxiety symptoms, it makes sense to see your anxiety as an expression of your "fear." So on your journey you'll move toward not only overcoming anxiety, but also that which you fear. More importantly, you'll learn how to outsmart your brain's false "fear messages."

I'm often asked by patients if I've ever personally struggled with anxiety. I usually smile and say very few people can become experts in anything without firsthand experience. Frankly, I've had just about every anxiety issue under the sun. There are few things in life that are quite profound. Defeating anxiety by facing and overcoming fear is one. Few experiences can simultaneously release, empower, enlighten, and inspire us like facing fear can.

I'm proud to say that by practicing all that I've included in these pages, I've overcome fears in the triple digits over the years. I even overcame a few in the midst of writing this book! I've faced fears both big and small. Many of them subjective, others more common, I suppose, in that a larger part of our population fears facing them, too. For example, I've been skydiving and scuba diving, taken a flight in a glider, gone parasailing, had countless public speaking engagements, officiated a wedding, been on live news, and even allowed an animal expert to place a tarantula on my head. And yet, there are and will be other fears to face. Some I'm familiar with and continue to work on, others are unknown and have yet to arrive. That is the nature of fear.

I believe that facing fear is one of life's purposes. For, in order to evolve, change, and grow, one must face fear. *You can learn a lot by this process. Lessons that can guide you throughout your life.* I'm not talking about facing fear from an ego standpoint—that's something else. And I'm not talking about being an adrenaline junkie/thrill seeker, either. That's also something else. Though, if you enjoy that, by all means! Facing fear is more about being on the journey to reach your potential and seek the truth.

I remember some years ago watching a reality show depicting climbers on their journey to reach the peak of Mount Everest. Many of them were climbing it for ego, it seemed. Still, a few others seemed to be in it for the journey and to reach their potential. Many were impeded by their physical condition. One person in particular, a firefighter, came very close, but had to stop. The biology of his body would not allow him to continue and struck him with altitude sickness. Though disappointed, his epiphany at that moment was he had reached his own personal Mount Everest. That was his peak. We all have our Everest. There are real struggles and limitations, and then there are those that are self-imposed that we allow to hinder us and our potential.

Anxiety isn't the enemy you believe it to be. In fact, your anxiety is communicating *with* you. It's most likely trying to tell you two things. First, that you've got something to learn. And second, that something needs to change.

In this book are the most successful techniques I've used over the past twenty-plus years to help hundreds of patients achieve complete reduction in anxious suffering. The techniques I'm referring to fall under the treatment classification of Cognitive-Behavioral Therapy (also known as CBT), which is different from most, if not all, other forms of anxiety treatment in that it's been scientifically proven to be effective.

Thankfully, though science-based, these techniques are easy to put into place. Anyone can face fear and extinguish their anxiety symptoms. The hard part is stepping into what scares you. This is no cause for alarm, though. This book provides gradual, easy-to-understand steps to do so, no matter how afraid you are.

In the pages to follow, we'll specifically be discussing anxiety in the form of phobias, panic attacks and obsessive-compulsive disorder (OCD). I've left out post-traumatic stress disorder (PTSD) because, though common, this falls outside the realm of a typical person's anxiety struggles. I've also refrained from discussing what my field calls generalized anxiety disorder (GAD), given that this diagnosis is a bit of a misnomer. Its symptoms are more stress-based and focused on real-life conflicts (e.g., financial woes, marital conflict, etc.), albeit ones that might be blown out of proportion, resulting in worry. That said, its symptom of worry *is* rooted in fear. Therefore, those with GAD can still benefit from the lessons in this book, especially those on imaginal exposure, false belief, and "What If" thoughts. So for you, GAD sufferers, feel free to read on. You'll receive plenty for your efforts, too.

In addition to "fear," you probably noticed that the subtitle of this book mentions the brain. You'll soon learn how your brain plays a massive foundational role in the manifestation and continuation of your anxiety symptoms. More importantly, you'll learn how to outsmart it by using *the* counterintuitive approach. I should say—so I will—that this book is in no way meant to be a treatise or comprehensive report on the brain's functions, interactions, and development related to anxiety. That would defeat the purpose of this book and is also better left to neurologists or neuropsychologists. This is a self-help book. My purpose is to teach you how to treat your anxiety on your own. What I've included is out of necessity, to inform you of both how you are encouraging your brain to generate anxiety, and more importantly, how you can outfox it!

Chapters 1 through 6 are geared toward providing you with anxiety getaway information, lessons, and techniques for you to start applying. The last three chapters (7, 8, and 9) are where you can pinpoint your own anxiety symptoms diagnostically and put all that you've learned together to easily create your personal self-help treatment plan. You might find that, because the last three chapters are focused on specific diagnoses, only one might apply to you. So when you arrive there, feel free to just read what resonates. Though if you're unsure of your diagnosis, it's probably best to read each chapter to support your quest. After all, you've got to know what you're dealing with to treat it! You might even find that they all apply, for it's not uncommon to have an anxiety trifecta! Conversely, you may find tips and info that do directly apply to you, even though the diagnostic label may not.

Once you put the techniques in this book into practice and reap the rewards, you'll have entered a new stage in handling your anxiety, and perhaps even in handling life's challenges. Simply put, you'll be in charge of eliminating the anxious suffering you experienced prior to your anxiety getaway. This book makes you captain of your own cruise ship.

But you must continue to practice your newfound skills! Anxiety resolution is not a one-and-done achievement. Life has its difficulties, its ups and downs. Fear can and will arise. But now you'll know exactly what to do when it does. And all you'll have to do is...do what you've learned!

In the upcoming pages, you'll learn more about what your anxiety is and what it isn't. You'll also learn how to outsmart your brain's false fear messages. Most importantly, you'll learn how to claim your calm and make your anxiety getaway!

Whether you believe it or not, you've already taken the first step. Now it's time to take a few more.

CHAPTER 1

ANXIETY VS. ANXIETY BON VOYAGE

"I am not afraid of storms, for I am learning how to sail my ship."

—Louisa May Alcott

Have you ever seen footage of a rattlesnake when it strikes? The anticipation is tremendous. And when it does strike, it is vicious in its speed, ferocity, and bite. This is what anxiety feels like for many. Of course, anxiety varies in intensity. But no matter the severity, people's struggle with anxiety always amounts to some degree of suffering. They suffer with their symptoms, the limitations anxiety places on their lives, the impact it has on their relationships, and because they are simply afraid.

When people call my center for help, they are often at the tipping point of "enough pain" to motivate them to seek *the* effective, healthy way out—no matter the challenge. This motivation can be the foundation of their breakthrough, and it is this motivation that I often call upon in my sessions with anxiety sufferers. Whether dealing with a phobia, panic attacks, or OCD, motivation is going to be required to overcome your anxiety symptoms. No ifs, ands, or buts about it. No reason to stress, though. This requirement is commonplace throughout life.

Motivation is always a factor in goal achievement. Achieving any goal of great meaning, plus one that offers a great sense of freedom, can be a challenge. And any worthwhile challenge requires time, effort, courage... and an appropriate dose of motivation to achieve it. That, plus maybe a latte or two.

I always notice people's demeanor when they enter my office for the first time. They are sometimes cautious, lest their high hopes get dashed. But that caution is coupled with excitement. Excitement over the bright and shiny object of what is, to them, a new anxiety treatment. Anything new (and don't forget scientifically proven!) in our eyes can bring us excitement. Cognitive-Behavioral Therapy (CBT) for anxiety is typically something people haven't tried before, and maybe something they've read is supposed to work. After their history of trying many different unproven, non-scientific methods, with little to no anxiety reduction, they are usually ready to jump in. I often enjoy this time with people because they're brimming with hope and motivation to do the work required (and willing to complete the homework I assign!).

Still, after over twenty years and hundreds of patients that I've helped overcome their symptoms, there are always some who display "the downturn" and stop before breaking free. Essentially, the downturn is a quick decline in motivation. For them, the bloom will soon be off the rose when it comes to walking the path of this treatment, the bright and shiny newness now gone. Why? Because soon they will be in the treatment grind, working on their anxiety with a proven, structured, and gradual plan. They've transitioned to the blah, tedious, Nike slogan-like "Just Do It" phase. It will no longer be exciting and it can be a little scary.

Facing fear takes some work. It can be a process that is no day at the beach—or if you're more of a dry land person, no walk in the park. I liken this treatment grind to getting in shape at the gym. Most who exercise consistently have made workouts part of their routine. After the excitement of a new gym, new workout class, or new trainer has worn off, you transition to the routine of working on a goal. Nothing exciting to see here, folks! Just *work* that, if consistent, will get you to your anxiety getaway. And that's where excitement reigns! If you want to conquer your anxiety symptoms, you've just got to be willing to grind it out for progress. Do the work to claim your calm!

Sometimes I'm still surprised to find that one of the biggest barriers to total anxiety reduction can rest on a little progress. Yes, you read that right. Sounds strange, doesn't it? But once some people with an attachment to the bright, shiny object of this proven treatment make some progress, they falter. Now a little bit happier and feeling a bit more freedom than they've experienced in a long time, they start to back off. Why? Because for many, the suffering that remains is tolerable. It's an acceptable amount of suffering because it's better than what they've been living with. Sadly, for some, this can mark the end of treatment, as they make the choice (and it is always a choice) to back away from totally ridding themselves of still limiting anxiety symptoms. Of course, the progress they've made is still positive. However, it's difficult not to see it as sad when one chooses to live life with ongoing anxiety symptoms that are resolvable, rather than completing the work required and living life with full freedom.

But why would anybody willingly accept any degree of anxious suffering? There must be a larger explanation than a desire to escape the treatment grind. It doesn't make logical sense. When valuable progress with these scientific, proven methods has been accomplished, why wouldn't one continue with the plan to reduce *all* suffering created by their anxiety symptoms? Why choose to live with any measure of the same old fears and limitations? There are many unhealthy reasons I've seen in my twenty-plus years in practice. Here are some:

1. Some people have grown accustomed to living with a daily dose of suffering. They're so used to it, in fact, that the uncertainty around not having their anxious symptoms can lead to more unconscious anxiety. In other words, they're afraid they wouldn't know what to do with themselves without

the symptoms they've built a life around!
What would they do with all that free time?

On a separate, but simultaneous, note: some
unconsciously also believe they deserve their suffering.
It's as if they believe they're not worthy of having a life
filled with freedom and joy without some form of self-
imposed torture. Talk about a false belief (we'll cover
these soon)!

2. Fear of losing one's identity is another issue
    that can lead to a premature departure
    from completing this anxiety treatment.
    When anxiety symptoms have been present
    for a long time and have become part of
    the fabric of one's daily life, they may be
    intertwined with one's identity. Even family
    members might now define "you" as your
    anxiety, based on the adjustments they've
    made for it over time.

This reminds me of a patient, Marisol, who saw herself
as "some kind of lunatic," as did her family! Marisol was
unaware she had severe OCD. In fact, prior to entering
my office, she had never sought treatment or any
diagnostic evaluation. Steeped in a germ obsession,
Marisol was suffering from a compulsive home practice
of laying down towels as stepping stones in order to
move from room to room. To her credit, at that time
she worked hard and was soon able to walk through
the kitchen and bedroom in her socks, free of towel
assistance. But then, abruptly, she quit treatment...
before attacking the bathrooms, living room, and
hallways. Based on our discussions in prior sessions,
it seemed that she and her family could not let go of
her assigned identity as a "crazy" person. The very idea
of what life would be like without that identity was

so threatening, she could not bear the uncertainty of finding out.

Allowing your identity to be wrapped up in your anxious symptoms is a big error. You are not your anxiety! But if you have done so, don't be alarmed. You're not the first and you won't be the last. And while there's no denying it can be scary to face the unknown, you'll learn how to live without your symptoms as you gradually overcome anxiety with the proven techniques in this book. Won't you welcome getting acquainted with that experience, and getting acquainted with the real "you"?

3. Secondary gains can be another unhealthy motivation as to why people quit treatment before breaking free from their anxiety symptoms. When it comes to anxiety, secondary gains are an indirect and often unconscious "benefit" of avoiding progress. Here's a simple example to clarify: I recall Evan, an unmotivated former patient, who mentioned with a smile that his family never asked him to pick them up at the airport due to his fear of driving. For Evan, it appeared that one secondary gain of maintaining his phobia was never being burdened with an airport pickup! A broader secondary gain may have been that few in the family sought his help for much of anything at all.

Sadly, people can develop an attachment to secondary gains. This, of course, can further destructive anxiety management behaviors and decrease motivation for progress. The costs of choosing secondary gains over anxiety reduction can be eye-opening. For example, people will start to expect less of you and, subsequently, you may begin to expect less of yourself.

Is it true that once your anxiety has lifted, people will expect more from you? Probably so. But don't you want them to? Shouldn't you expect more from yourself? Your anxiety has not only placed barriers on your life, but maybe also on the lives of loved ones. You owe it to yourself (and perhaps to them) to move beyond your anxiety symptoms.

4. The last, and perhaps most obvious, reason people quit treatment is (this one is worthy of a drum roll)...FEAR. They're simply afraid to fully face their anxiety, so they don't continue to use these proven techniques. Some even decide their anxiety symptoms are meant to be, and never try making progress again.

When people quit based on fear, they miss the chance to discover that this fear barrier is not as difficult to conquer as they think. Why? Because the steps provided in this book can be taken very gradually. You can set the pace. If feeling afraid or even terrified, you can go as slow as you need. It's always best to start where you are. Wherever you are is *your* beginning. Don't judge yourself or accept some false belief that you're weak and should be further along. By using the scientifically proven tools in this book, you can make steady progress, no matter your degree of fear—if you allow it. If you accept the help and choose to help yourself. If you commit. Your choice.

A Caution and Word of Encouragement to All Reading This Book

See your anxiety symptom reduction through to the end. You must do this if you want the relief and freedom you deserve. As you learn the techniques in this book and begin to apply them, you'll make progress. Reject anxious suffering as your lot in life and keep pushing forward. No one needs to live with anxiety symptoms. You deserve much more! Why accept suffering that is unnecessary? Life offers enough challenges that are fully out of our control. Don't give up the fight. This is a fight you can absolutely win.

Clichés for transcending fear and taking the necessary steps abound. You've heard many, such as "Journey of a thousand miles...," "No risk, no reward," "Every bit of forward movement is progress," "Just keep moving the ball down the field," and more. That's because they're all true. So just take the steps... Commit to the journey... Keep putting one foot in front of the other... And be brave. You'll discover you're stronger than you ever knew as you walk the path of becoming a fear-facing warrior.

CHAPTER 2

WHAT IS ANXIETY, REALLY?

"Of all the liars in the world, sometimes the worst are our own fears."

—Rudyard Kipling

"High anxiety, it's always the same."

—Mel Brooks, as sung in the film
High Anxiety

Anxiety is most easily defined by its emotional, mental, and physical symptoms. On the emotional end, most of my patients over the years have described their anxiety as a bad feeling, one of impending doom, unease, tension, or restlessness. On the mental side, thoughts of losing control, intense worry, or "what if?" wreak havoc. And on the physical front, anxiety can manifest in a myriad of symptoms, from flop sweat to rapid heartbeat, with a full range of degrees and freak-out reactions.

Those that suffer with anxiety know these symptoms well. And their family members, spouses, romantic partners and friends are familiar with them, too, having seen their loved one's struggle. However, much to the exasperation of the anxiety sufferer, their seeing does not often mean believing. And, certainly not often understanding. In fact, this can be a huge frustration for the anxiety sufferer, one that those who have never struggled with anxiety *just don't get.*

Casey, a former patient of mine, was infuriated with her husband for not understanding the abject terror of her panic attacks. "He just gives me this look like I'm weak. Like he doesn't know what to do with me or for me. Like I'm a child. It feels so judgmental and condescending. He must think I'm making up my panic on purpose. Some need for attention. Or drama. He doesn't understand because he can be like a robot. His emotions are always steady. I don't wish my anxiety on anybody, but if he could just have it for a day, then he'd get it."

Casey's desire for her husband's understanding became an unnecessary focus and created conflict in her marriage. It also exacerbated her anxiety symptoms. She was finally able to give up her pointless, five-year "make my husband get it" quest by adopting these two reality-based beliefs.

Reality-Based Belief #1

For those that don't struggle with anxiety, trying to understand the experience is like a man trying to understand what it's like to be pregnant. Sure, a man can see that the extra weight has the potential to hurt a woman's back. He can also appreciate, intellectually, that pregnancy can involve morning sickness. But men will never truly understand the pregnant experience because it's one of those experiences in life that, to truly understand it, you must go through it firsthand. Same goes for an anxiety syndrome.

Reality-Based Belief #2

Your anxiety struggle and the process of overcoming it is yours to own. After all, it is *your* anxiety. By all means, try to receive understanding. Seek support from your loved ones. Get hugs. But if they don't understand, it really doesn't matter, because no loved one can assist you in resolving your anxiety symptoms. If understanding and support from family and friends is offered and available, great. That said, though nice, support from family and friends is not needed. What is needed are scientifically proven anxiety treatment strategies to point you to freedom's path. But no one can walk the path for you. And you'll be amazed at the empowerment you can feel by walking it yourself. Progress made by you, and yours to keep.

Whether on your own or with your loved ones' support, no matter if anybody in your life actually "gets it," to make your anxiety getaway, it must first be made clear that...

ANXIETY IS FEAR

They are one and the same. You can't have anxiety without fear. Anxiety means you are afraid. In considering the hundreds and hundreds of anxiety-ridden patients I've treated over twenty years, there was never a person whose anxiety did not represent fear.

But do you know specifically what you fear?

To beat your anxiety, you need to identify the road block. How can you resolve your symptoms if it's unclear what you fear (potential song lyric?)?

I worked with a young woman in her late twenties named Sadie who, in her first session, described her debilitating anxiety while both standing in line at the grocery store and shopping at Target in the back aisles. Complicating matters, she was unaware of what she feared. To cope, she simply avoided these errands. This led to a scarcity of essentials in the house, one of which being toilet paper. Sadie started to lean on friends and her sister to bring her these items. I doubt any of them ever expected to be her Charmin supplier!

Through some exploration, we identified that while in line at the grocery store, Sadie felt unable to leave with a full cart. She felt trapped. And when shopping deep in the back aisles of Target, she felt like she was on a deserted island. With a mix of fear and frustration, Sadie proclaimed, "I can't even see the exit!"

It's not always easy to identify a fear because the extreme nature of some anxiety symptoms can pull focus, masking the fear itself. But attempting to resolve anxiety symptoms without addressing one's actual fear would be like treating a broken arm without addressing the fracture. If unaware of the break, one might simply ice the swelling, when successful treatment actually calls for a cast. This works against creating the correct fear-focused plan to truly break free. And you waste a lot of time.

So, the first step in making your anxiety getaway is identifying what you fear. That said, let's begin to turn the tables on your anxiety by looking it in the eye.

How to Determine What You Fear

1. Mentally recreate the image or experience of what triggers your anxiety symptoms. For example, I began by encouraging Sadie to imagine herself in the back aisles of Target.

2. Ask yourself, "What does the experience feel like?", "What do I hope won't happen?", "What do I dislike about this situation?" These questions provoked anxiety in Sadie. She responded with, "It feels like I can't leave. And I'm not a fan of being too deep in any store. Especially a big warehouse type like Target. I don't want to feel stuck. I hate when my hands shake. I feel short of breath and dizzy."

3. Ask yourself, "Is it the experience I fear, or do I have anxiety based on a 'What if' thought?" (as in, "What if...happens?"). Sadie was plagued by thoughts such as, "What if I can't get out of Target fast enough? What if I panic?"

4. If anxiety is triggered in more than one situation, ask yourself if there is a *common theme* during these moments. What do they all share, if anything, or are they separate? Although those who struggle with anxiety can have multiple fears, people with a complex phobia (something we'll discuss more of later) fear one or two major themes. And these greatest hits are played ad nauseam! For example, Sadie shared that she felt anxiety in line at the grocery store and at Target. She added that she felt anxiety in traffic and elevators, too. We quickly identified the common theme as a fear of being trapped while believing a fast escape was difficult or impossible. This fear (and Sadie's anxiety symptoms) led me to her diagnosis of agoraphobia. I then created her treatment plan accordingly.

What Anxiety is NOT

* A phase: An anxiety disorder is not some child-like developmental difficulty that will vanish on its own.

* Something you can distract or breathe your way out of: You've probably already tried these ineffective strategies.

* A disease: It's not like the flu. You're not stricken by anxiety, and you're no leper for having it either!

* Personal: It's not your identity. It's a brain issue.

* What you deserve: You're not being punished, though it might feel this way.

* Your destiny: No one is destined for a life filled with anxiety (unless they choose not to follow the proper strategies to overcome it).

* The end of days.

A Dip in Your Family's Gene Pool?

Your anxiety most likely has genetic roots. For example, many people that I treat at my center tend to have a family history of phobias, panic attack struggles, or OCD. The genetic connection can be close and obvious, like a parent, or less direct, like a second aunt or a great grandfather. To put it simply, this means that those with anxious wiring tend to be more prone to potential anxiety issues than those without. However, this propensity for developing an anxiety issue by no means suggests that it's a foregone conclusion. It just means the table has been set, should you take certain actions to sit down and eat! This is analogous to someone with a genetic predisposition toward alcohol abuse. Even though the pull might be strong, you only become an alcoholic once you abuse alcohol.

Now this might come as a surprise...

ANXIETY IS ALSO AN ILLUSION

Most respond defensively to this construct, at first. They often remark, "But it feels real. Shouldn't I trust my feelings? Don't my feelings matter?"

I'm not dismissing how you feel. As a psychologist, I'm willing and able to validate anxious feelings. Just don't ask me to validate parking! But my validating your anxious feelings only goes as far as offering understanding that you feel the way you do. Again, I'm not dismissing how or what you feel. Struggling with anxiety symptoms can be a challenge, at best. At worst, anxiety can be so destructive that it shuts down a life (only with your avoidance and without the tools in this book, of course). So allow me to clarify this "anxiety is an illusion" statement...

ANXIETY IS YOUR BRAIN'S FALSE FEAR MESSAGE

That's right. There's no real danger. But there is danger in the false fear message you're reinforcing and hearing loud and clear. So we'll be discussing how to outsmart these messages in detail, in short order.

Anxiety Getaway Tip

Your anxiety symptoms can't kill you. Here's some proof: Ask yourself how many times you've been anxious. How many times have you experienced these anxiety symptoms? And yet, here you sit reading this book. So, anxiety symptoms can't kill you. They can, however, make life rather unpleasant.

Reading this book demonstrates your readiness to break free from anxiety's grip and move forward. So congratulations! You're taking the first important step toward living with more freedom, opportunity, and joy. And on that note, let's move forward.

CHAPTER 3

YOUR BRAIN ON ANXIETY

"It takes brains..."

—Unknown author

"More brains..."

—Zombie from *The Return of the Living Dead*

In order to make your anxiety getaway by freeing yourself of anxiety symptoms, it's vital that you first consider how the anxiety plane achieves lift off. Using this flying analogy, think of anxiety as having two separate, but connected, engine pieces. Your belief system is one. It plays a large, influential role. The other engine piece can be filled with vats of plane fuel and is, in large part, even more responsible for anxiety lift off. Yep, I'm talking about your brain.

BOARDING THE ANXIOUS BRAIN PLANE

Your anxiety is primarily a brain issue. It's not really about you. Still, it's easy to take anxiety personally because it sure does *feel* like you. After all, they're *your* anxious thoughts, feelings, reactions, and symptoms, right? At least that's what you tell yourself—it's what everybody who suffers from anxiety tells themselves. You're in the company of millions. Feel better? Probably not. Anxious misery does not love anxious company.

So how is anxiety a brain issue, exactly?

To answer that, we first need to talk about the biological gift that keeps on giving. It's called...

The Survival Instinct

We've all got one. It's part of the genius of our built-in biology. And it's designed to save our lives, when necessary. The most basic expression of our survival instinct is the fight-or-flight response. It is this biological mechanism that could be responsible for the perpetuation of our species back in caveman times (or "caveperson times," to bring it around to the twenty-first century). Without the fight-or-flight response, early men and women may never have survived all the hyena attacks (supposedly, that was a thing!) where they instinctually had to fight to the death or run like hell to stay alive. Getting an up-close-and-personal view of hyena choppers triggered their biology to kick in, with their adrenal gland releasing the hormone of adrenaline that prepared their body to fight or run.

Now back to the twenty-first century...

When it comes to the survival instinct in our regular, workaday lives, most of us are rarely faced with life-or-death situations (no, your in-laws don't count as hyenas). But for those who struggle with anxiety, their life is threatened on a daily basis. Well, not exactly, but that's what their brain is telling them. In actuality, their survival instinct is being erroneously triggered in the face of no real danger, just perceived danger.

In our twenty-first century daily lives, we rarely need our survival instinct triggered for protection. For example, a man afraid of small spaces steps on an elevator and his survival instinct springs forth with its adrenalized alarm bells. Something is wrong here, though most can see there's no life-or-death situation at hand. So, what...is... happening?

This man's survival instinct has gone haywire! His brain is sending his system false fear messages, triggering his fight-or-flight response. But why? Shouldn't his brain conclude that there is no real threat present and delete these messages? Ideally, yes. Unfortunately, our brains can have trouble distinguishing between real danger and false danger.

Consider a darkened theater. You sit, riveted by the screen. Your popcorn-buttered hand trembles with fear. Your lip quivers. Maybe some beads of sweat form. You want to yell, "Look out! That googly-eyed demon is around the corner!" Are you in any actual demon danger? Is anyone? No, you're in an air conditioned theater munching on popcorn, sipping soda, and watching a film. And yet, our bodies experience adrenaline.

In addition to our brain's less than stellar ability to distinguish real-life danger from perceived danger, there is another explanation for our survival instinct's triggering error. In this day and age, replete with constant change and advancements in modern technology, that explanation can be summed up in one word...

Pressure.

In North America, our survival instincts can be triggered by the pressures and expectations of our family, environment, and society alone. For example, even now, many still see the achievement of "The American Dream" as marriage, a house and 2.2 kids. This common expectation in itself continues to place a stressful burden on the many young adults in pursuit of it, and the older adults whose lives don't match up. The pressure to achieve this so-called ideal can lead to interpreting any barrier as a threat to one's well-being, stability, and yes, survival. Even on a small scale, it's easy to see how one can interpret a minor event as a crisis with this pressure in play. For instance, say you get a flat tire on your way to work, rendering you late. This just happens to be a day that you're due to present data alongside other colleagues you happen to be competing with for a promotion. The inherent pressure based on the promise of "The American Dream" suggests that this flat tire will now affect your entire future. Your mind is inundated with thoughts like, "Now I won't get the promotion because my boss will think less of me, my colleagues will have a chance to impress her, and they'll all go on to great success and happiness. Meanwhile, I'll be stuck in this dissatisfying job, living in a place I despise, with no relationship potential to speak of and no prospects due to my inability to offer anybody much of anything. So, I better fix this flat tire in five minutes or my life and I are toast."

Aaaaaaaahhhhhhh! That is one pressure-filled flat tire!

And this flat tire scenario is only one of many pressures demonstrating how we can misinterpret barriers, whether perceived or real, as threats to our well-being, livelihood, and life. And it is these misinterpretations that can trigger a brain to respond with the fight-or-flight adrenaline surge, which leads to false fear messages that are perpetuated by those struggling with anxiety.

How many perceived threats and pressures do you encourage on a daily basis that set the stage for your brain's false fear messages?

Some Common Family and Societal Pressures Many of Us Perpetuate

* Need for great friends and acceptance by peers

* Need for clarity of direction and purpose in life (education, career pursuit, etc.)

* Having a "good" body

* Loving yourself or having a good self-esteem

* Wearing fashionable clothing

* Advancement in career, plus respect of boss and coworkers

* Need to maintain a youthful appearance

* Finding the "right" romantic partner to avoid being "alone"

* Marriage by a certain age

* Earning a bigger income

* Driving a status-oriented car

* Keeping up with the Joneses

With approximately 275 million people around the globe struggling with an anxiety disorder,[1] it seems like few places on Earth are immune to anxiety.

US statistics suggest that one in thirteen people struggle with anxiety.[2] In addition to the common genetic predisposition described in chapter 2, the most likely reason for anxiety is the influence of our society's expectations, pressures, and desires.

That said, ultimately we as individuals are responsible for pulling our brain's anxiety trigger, not any societal pressure. And by accepting responsibility for your anxiety's creation, you can also empower yourself with the accountability to extinguish it. I know it's a drag for most of us to hold ourselves accountable for our mental health, but if we want to be healthy, properly functioning adults living a life of freedom, it's the way there.

We'll discuss how to put out your anxiety fire by outsmarting your brain's false fear messages soon. For now, it's important for you to understand that you're unintentionally encouraging your brain's transmittal of these messages, setting yourself up to stimulate trouble with a capital A (for anxiety, that is).

Your No-Nonsense Brain/ Anxiety Breakdown

Neurologically speaking, the creation of anxiety is challenging to pinpoint. In the scientific community, neurobiological researchers, such as Dr. Martin, Dr. Ressler, Dr. Binder, and Dr. Nemeroff, attribute the basis of this anxiety complex to the involvement of neurotransmitters and neuroanatomy, along with their strong link to circuits in the limbic system, brain stem, and higher cortical brain areas.[3] Still, even with anxiety's sophisticated neurological nature, there is a widely accepted, straightforward view. For the sake of clarity (and also because you've probably got a lot on your mind!), we'll consider the brain/ anxiety breakdown from this straightforward view, too. Here we go...

The first step toward the manifestation of anxiety begins when *any* thought or event occurs and we misinterpret it as a threat. This triggers the limbic system of our brain, where most of our feelings are molded. I suppose that's why it's known as the hub of emotion. The parts of this hub most associated with anxiety are the amygdala and the hypothalamus.

The amygdala's role is to process stimuli and respond with emotion.[4] In fact, Dr. Richter-Levin and Dr. Akirav have confirmed that the amygdala is the most specifically engaged brain structure both in emotional responses and in the development of emotional memories.[5] More specifically with regard to anxiety, Dr. Martin and her colleagues found that the amygdala formulates fear while establishing fear-based memories. Whether interpreted correctly or not, when the amygdala grasps danger, it sends a warning to the hypothalamus.[6] The hypothalamus then notifies the sympathetic nervous system.[7] Pretty heady stuff!

The sympathetic nervous system revs your body up like a biker at a Hell's Angels' mixer, sparking the adrenal gland, which produces the adrenaline response! That's what you feel when you're feeling anxious, though lots of activity behind the scenes is in effect.

The adrenaline response creates a host of systemic actions, such as increased energy, maximized concentration, improved reflexes, a quickened heart beat to propel more blood to the muscles to make you stronger, focused vision, and more. This process helps us when we need to protect ourselves from a legit danger. However—and this should not be a shocker at this point—this brain process can hurt us when we misinterpret danger. This misinterpretation sets our brains into anxiety mode by attaching fear-based thoughts, beliefs, and stories to safe or neutral things, and that encourages the adrenaline response. And the brain, having learned this fallacious lesson of danger, repeatedly encourages the adrenaline response when confronted by those particular "dangerous" stimuli. And what would you say this means the brain is now providing? That's right, boys and girls—an ongoing pattern of false fear messages!

But the adrenal gland isn't only activated in the face of perceived danger. Remember, the amygdala is the brain's emotional reaction center. It processes other intense emotions,[8] including excitement and uncertainty. Working together with the amygdala, the hypothalamus responds to these emotions as it would to anxiety, by engaging the sympathetic nervous system to prepare the body for effort.[9] This can account for adrenaline without fear. Unfortunately, when the adrenaline response is triggered by excitement or uncertainty, people with a genetic neurological predisposition to anxiety often misinterpret it as... anxiety. Again, it is this misinterpretation that establishes triggers for anxiety along with the subsequent beliefs attached to the experience.

So the differences between excitement-based adrenaline, uncertainty-based adrenaline, and fear-based adrenaline are not necessarily physiological, but psychological. They are perspective-driven. Adrenaline is adrenaline! In other words, the differences are not in the adrenaline itself, but are predicated on how one perceives their adrenaline response in a specific situation. For example, if you were about to skydive out of an airplane for the first time, you might feel terrified. For an experienced skydiver on their fiftieth jump, the feeling could be described by any word synonymous with "wee!" or "yahoo!" Same adrenaline, differently labeled.

In any given moment, if you misinterpret excitement or uncertainty-based adrenaline as fear, you will be anxious. As such, you will then most likely label the context in which you experienced this adrenaline as dangerous and continue to be afraid. For example, Iris often felt anxious arriving at parties, though it wasn't due to a social phobia. The truth is, she didn't know why she suffered such party dread. With treatment, Iris soon accepted that parties can be fraught with uncertainty over who you might meet or whether you'll enjoy yourself as the evening progresses. She had been misinterpreting her uncertainty-based adrenaline as a threat, which sent her off to the anxiety races! The more she misinterpreted this threat, the more intimidating parties became. And the more she fought "party anxiety," the more she taught her brain to protect her from "dangerous parties" with an even bigger adrenaline wave. By adding additional scary false beliefs to this process, like "I can't take the noise and chaos at parties," she created a monster of a party phobia!

For the most part, your misinterpretation of danger is the fuel for anxiety. Following consistent, specific misinterpretations of danger, the brain is the engine that drives that struggle deeper, until one walks the right path to undo the cycle created by anxiety. These misinterpretations are generally synonymous with false beliefs. We'll discuss the importance of changing our false beliefs, along with strategies on how to do so, in detail in a later chapter.

High this is obvious.

For now, understanding your brain's role in anxiety is a big step toward making your anxiety getaway! In fact, this understanding fast tracks you to the key strategy on outsmarting your brain's false fear messages to make that very getaway. This strategy is called "exposure."

Read on!

IT'S IN THE LABELING

Although our survival instinct, accompanied by its adrenaline release, can be triggered by unfamiliar situations, it's the false danger labels we assign these situations that encourage anxiety. For example, eager actors who are about to go onstage for the opening night of a play experience adrenaline. But they don't call it "panic," or consider it "dangerous" or "wrong." They call their adrenalized experience "butterflies." And their "butterflies" label is based on the manner in which they accept the excitement of the evening along with the uncertainty over how the play will be received. Performing in front of a crowd is their jam!

How you label your adrenaline experience is key. Trouble arises when you label an adrenaline surge as "wrong," "bad," "terrible," or just something that should most definitely *not* be happening. Granted, when your system is flooded with adrenaline in a situation that most would agree does not warrant it, there can be confusion. It doesn't seem to make sense. This confusion propels the mind to ask, "Why? Why am I feeling this way? What is happening to me?" For instance, if you're driving home from work on a route that you've taken daily for years and, suddenly, your system is flooded with adrenaline, it's natural to question it. Unfortunately, the untreated anxiety sufferer attaches a self-defeating label or scary story to this surge—the opening line likely being some version of, "Oh no. Something is definitely wrong."

To repeat, although your biological inclination is to avoid discomfort, it's your "scary" labeling of the uncomfortable experience that sets this whole anxiety monster in motion. The biological inclination is part of what makes us human. The error is indulging it with your anxious creative narrative in the face of misperceived danger.

Jeffrey, a man in his late twenties, feared the night. He said he just didn't like the way it made him feel. This began one evening when he became ill. He said it might've occurred after eating a cheeseburger. All he remembered was that he felt sick, it was uncomfortable, it was night, and he didn't like it.

What Jeffrey didn't know following this short, mysterious illness, was that he taught his brain to fear the night by avoiding going out after sundown.

BOOM! Hello, nighttime anxiety, or so-called fear of the dark (a.k.a. nyctophobia).

The more Jeffrey avoided going out at night, the more he taught his brain that night was "bad." Night was dangerous. And, more specifically, that night would make him ill. You might ask, "Why didn't he develop a fear of cheeseburgers instead?" It's anybody's guess. This is the nature of irrational fear. Because Jeffrey believed the discomfort of feeling ill was intolerable, he sought an explanation and fell on "the night," due to the timing of his illness. And like brains do when lacking more specific, relevant data, Jeffrey's brain gave him an unfortunate assist by making a quick association.

Though seemingly efficient, this energy-saving brain tactic often leads to errors.

Beyond his perspective, why would Jeffrey label "feeling ill" as horrendous, rather than just unpleasant? Objectively, there was no emergency. No major threat to his survival. So what gives?

First, based on a longstanding pattern of avoiding discomfort, Jeffrey had developed a low frustration tolerance. Feeling ill was uncomfortable, and this discomfort for Jeffrey *was* intolerable. So he searched for a way to run from it.

But more importantly, the unknown itself can be uncomfortable. Ability to tolerate the unknown is a major factor in the degree of anxiety struggle for any individual. Think about a person you know who rarely struggles with anxiety. A person who almost never seems anxious. Typically, they have a strong ability to tolerate the unknown (we'll discuss how this can be cultivated soon).

Jeffrey had a limited ability to tolerate the unknown, due to his pattern of fighting experiences where he was uncertain of the outcome. Of course, certainty of an outcome is never an option. Even when we expect an outcome based on a consistent result pattern, it can still change. For years, I fed our dog dry food. Then one day he refused to eat without my adding some wet dog food to the mix. I was certain that wouldn't happen. It never had before, therefore it wasn't supposed to happen at present. Try telling that to a hungry, salivating canine!

There is no certainty, just varying degrees of uncertainty. For Jeffrey that night, the uncertainty was, "Why do I feel ill?" He searched and searched for an answer, to no avail. When no clear cut answer was available, he fell upon "night," led by his overwhelming desire to make the unknown...known. And when he avoided going out one evening for fear of feeling ill again, he taught his brain that "night" was a dangerous experience. That darkness was a hazardous and probable risk to his survival. The more he avoided it, the worse his fear of night became.

AVOIDANCE IS THE ENEMY

Whenever you avoid what you fear, you forge a neural pathway within your brain that associates the fear-inducing stimuli with a threat to your survival. In other words, you are erroneously teaching your brain to protect you from that stimuli via your survival instinct's fight-or-flight response. The more you avoid what you fear, the deeper that groove in your brain becomes (a deep groove, but definitely not groovy!). The deeper the groove of this self-created neural pathway, the more often it takes you to a place of anxiety whenever triggered by the fear-inducing stimuli to which you've now developed an association. This is all unintentional on your part, of course. No need to start beating yourself up. It won't help anyway. You were simply adhering to your biological inclination to seek pleasure and avoid pain. However, now it's time to turn your life around and claim your calm. Enough of these needless fears with their time-wasting anxiety symptoms!

One of the biggest challenges in overcoming fear is that, although the brain learns lessons quickly, it does not *unlearn* lessons quickly. Ever traveled by train? On every trip, trains obey the direction of the tracks. If an engineer wanted to take the train in a different direction, but lacked the track, it would not be possible. New tracks would be necessary to divert the train onto a new course. And once a train has a destination on a track, it churns with momentum. The challenge lies in laying the new track. Like most goals in life, it would take patience, effort, and commitment to build that new path.

There is a similar challenge in facing anxiety and changing your brain's chemistry. In other words, creating a new neural pathway that is unafraid of what you currently fear is going to take some effort. But it can absolutely be done. You can change your brain's response to your anxiety-provoking stimulus by creating a new neural pathway (or laying new brain train tracks).

This might seem daunting. But just as all of our brains can be taught fear, they also have the capacity to unlearn fear. Our brain's ability to do so lies in its neuroplasticity. For over forty years, there have been research studies proving the brain's neuroplasticity, which is defined as the brain's ability to affect changes in brain regions, neuron linkages, and associations. Research has even proven over time that the brain can engender new neurons by a process called "neurogenesis."[10] So what does this mean for outsmarting your brain's false fear messages? It means you can generate calm in the face of your anxiety by changing how your brain perceives and experiences its triggers via specific actions—the very actions we'll be discussing in short order!

Generally speaking, if you set something in motion in one direction, you can send it in another direction, too! Remember "the law of inertia" lesson in high school? I, myself, may have been asleep during that one. Let's refresh: In 1687, Sir Isaac Newton (of gravity fame) proved that a body or an object will continue moving in the direction it's moving until it is acted upon with force to redirect its movement.[11] So to overcome anxiety, you're going to have to expend some effort redirecting rather than avoiding.

THE SEDUCTIVE NATURE OF AVOIDANCE

Anxiety isn't sexy, but its avoidance is seductive. How do you stop yourself from avoiding anxiety when it feels so good in the moment? Most people would agree that when you avoid the very experience that brings you terror, you obtain great relief. Problem solved... Not! There is no real relief and no problem solved when avoidance is involved (Go ahead and sing this phrase, you know you want to!).

Avoidance is made of smoke and mirrors. Magicians often use smoke and mirrors to hide their tricks from the audience and blur reality. Should the audience see beyond the smoke and mirrors, reality would lead to disappointment for a lot of magic fans. The reality of avoiding anxiety will lead to disappointment, too. Avoidance is not only seductive, but deceptive. It urges your mind to believe you're seeing something that you're not. That something is relief.

Through avoidance, you always fortify what you fear. Always. It's unintentional on your part, of course. You don't mean to solidify your struggle. You're just looking for a way out of your anxiety prison. And the seductive nature of avoidance is hard to resist. Avoidance is a little like the Venus fly trap. Its beauty draws prey in, then its fangs eat it whole. Yikes!

Pete, an affable, good-looking guy in his late thirties, had been single all his life. At thirty-nine, he began to question if he'd be alone for the rest of it. He now hoped for a girlfriend, but had no idea what attaining this goal would entail. He had never had one. He was only familiar with one-night stands. He never learned how to truly connect with a woman, other than through quick and easy physical intimacy. This was now leaving him empty and unfulfilled.

Pete arrived in my office feeling lost. He described his recent attempts at dating with the purpose of developing a relationship, but he didn't know how to relate to women. Specifically, it made him anxious to discuss anything during a date due to a self-described absence in communication skills. Sure, he could charm women at bars with small talk. But when it came to substance or a true intimate moment, he felt powerless.

During his dates, women clued in fast on Pete's inability to address any deep subject matter. He believed this rendered him non-relationship material in their eyes. "I clam up when women start to ask me questions about my life. I try to answer, but I don't know what to say. I definitely don't want to talk about my father skipping out on us when I was ten. Or my alcoholic mother. Plus, I know they're expecting me to ask them things and listen to their problems. I think they want me to ask questions that show I care. But I honestly don't even know how. It makes me too nervous. I start sweating and stammering. I think they're immediately turned off. I've only gotten to a second date once in my life. She seemed as nervous as I was, but after that second date, she never texted me back. When I have a fair amount of alcohol in me, small talk is easy. Women don't seem to expect you to have a meaningful conversation at a bar. That's where I'm most comfortable. A few drinks in, I'm not worried about how women perceive me. I mean, who cares, right? I'll never see them again. I've actually started back at the bars. I think I'm gonna cancel my online dating apps. I might not be cut out for a relationship. Maybe I should just accept that and give up."

Though he was a bit misguided, I gave kudos to Pete for the attempt to challenge his brain's false fear messages by going on dates. I reiterated that, through avoidance, he had long ago taught his brain that dating and intimacy were dangerous. I then asked Pete how long he had been dating with the goal of working toward a relationship. Resigned, he said, "Over two months, with about one date every week. So, maybe eight dates." So much for commitment!

When I asked if he'd been modifying his dating routine based on lessons learned, he needed clarification. I explained that examining one date's responses to questions he asked could provide observational data to apply on subsequent dates. For example, if Pete asked about a woman's family with interest and she leaned in, then shared, that question would suggest a positive step toward connecting. Pete could then incorporate this question as connection practice during dates. In effect, this would challenge his brain's false fear messages rather than foster them. I asked again, this time more directly, if he changed his behavior at all during these eight dates. "No, I was just trying to survive the dates. I was mostly hoping my hands wouldn't shake or that I didn't look too nervous."

It struck me that although Pete believed he was afraid of intimacy, it seemed what Pete truly feared was potential criticism and rejection. This resonated with Pete. "I think that's right. I'm constantly trying to avoid caring about a woman because if I do and she criticizes me or breaks up with me, I'd be crushed. I suppose that's why spending time with women I have no real interest in is easier." Pete's fears of criticism and rejection are a main theme of social anxiety. The centralized pattern being attempts to avoid judgment, criticism, and rejection—often at all costs.

By running from his fear, Pete encouraged more fear. In other words, by avoiding asking questions during a date (and avoiding dating entirely for most of his life), Pete reinforced his fear. Thus, his avoidance continued to teach his brain that real intimacy could lead to terrible risk of judgment, criticism, and rejection. As a faithful student, his brain continued to trigger his fight-or-flight mechanism when in situations with potential to connect on a sincere level. All in all, Pete taught his brain to send false fear messages to his system, preparing Pete for mortal danger. So when faced with possible closeness, his body flooded with adrenaline, which in turn he interpreted as anxiety. The more Pete avoided asking questions, the more fearful he became. His brain then continued to send false fear messages, maintaining this cycle, much to Pete's dismay.

The science-proven, effective way of outsmarting your brain's false fear messages is never via the push of avoidance, but through a counterintuitive pull.

In chapters to follow, we'll talk about how to stop yourself from avoiding anxiety, so you can finally make your anxiety getaway and claim your calm. But for now, it's crucial you understand that your avoidance is maintaining your anxiety. And not only maintaining, but encouraging it, reinforcing it, and ensuring that it's going to cause you to suffer. Avoiding anxiety is ultimately like inviting someone you despise into your home and then advocating for their lengthy stay. Totally irrational, right?

Moving on...

Pete's focus on trying to survive dating without appearing anxious leads us to another manner in which one elicits false fear messages. In fact, it happens to be how anxiety is born!

Drumroll, please...

IN THE BEGINNING, THERE WAS "THE BATTLE"

An anxiety problem is created through your fighting it. It's created through the battle you try to survive, hoping that what you consider a hate-filled, terrifying torturer will flee, never to return. But like *Star Trek*'s infamous enemy The Borg says, "Resistance is futile!" Futile and destructive.

In his book *White Bears and Other Unwanted Thoughts*, Daniel Wegner, PhD, described the results of his innovative research on thought resistance. His experiments demonstrated that after instructing subjects not to think of white bears during the specified trials, they were unable to stop their brain from entertaining thoughts overflowing with these little white bears.[12] Dr. Wegner's experiments are a great example of the reality of battling anxiety. Who hasn't thought something unpleasant and found that the more they tried to stop thinking about it, the more they thought about it? These findings also support the spiritually-grounded adage "What you resist, persists."

Keep in mind, too, that when you fight anxiety, you create a certain conflict-based energy, the same as when you fight any externally-based conflict in the world. Conflict is a kind of energy, and energy is key to life. So by fighting anxiety, you're giving it life. Basically, you're Dr. Frankenstein creating your very own monster. And in the words of Dr. Frankenstein, "It's alive! It's alive!"

Your Brain's False Fear Message Process—in a Nutshell

1. An uncomfortable experience or thought occurs.

2. You teach your brain to fear this experience or thought by either...

   a. Doing what you can to avoid facing stimuli that trigger this experience or thought.

      OR...

   b. By fighting anxious thoughts and symptoms. (Often people do both.)

3. Following your teachings, your brain learns that this experience or thought is something to be feared. Hence, it deems it dangerous to your survival and seeks to protect you with your biological survival instinct whenever you're confronted with this anxious experience, whether in thought or in the actual world.

4. When confronted by this experience, your survival instinct activates its fight-or-flight mechanism. This mechanism now floods your system with adrenaline, preparing your body to duel to the death or bolt like a track star to save your life.

5. You interpret your adrenaline surge as an indicator of mortal danger. Your interpretation includes an anxiety-based story. For example, "I can't handle this. I'm going to lose my job because of this anxiety whenever I have to speak in a meeting."

6. The more you avoid and battle your particular anxiety-inducing event, the more you solidify the lesson neurologically. In other words, you strengthen the neural pathway that connects your feared event to a question of your survival.

7. Now, whenever you approach your fearful stimuli, your brain floods your system with adrenaline and you associate this with fear. You then indulge in your accompanying fear-based thoughts. And you become anxious again!

8. It goes around and around, like a vicious feedback loop. One experience impacts the other. You become anxious and you fight or run from anxiety. This creates more anxiety as you dodge and resist, again and again.

At this point, it's important for you to understand that anxiety is reinforced by avoidance and thrives through your fighting it. Through your battle against it. Through your resistance. If this isn't crystal clear yet, it will be once you begin practicing the counterintuitive tools to follow. So to learn how to outsmart your brain's false fear messages and claim your calm, just read on...

CHAPTER 4

ANOTHER SHOT OF ADRENALINE

"For an impressionist to paint from nature is not to paint the subject, but to realize sensations."

—Paul Cezanne

"I was an overnight sensation."

—Elvis

It's important to emphasize that an adrenaline surge does not equal anxiety. However, it does often manifest as anxiety for so many anxiety sufferers, especially if one has attached a fear-based story to both the sensations and the attempts to fight their existence. As mentioned, this battle leads to hypervigilance—purposely seeking out said sensations—with the counterproductive goal of trying to force them out of being. In a nutshell, if you're looking for trouble internally, you're going to find it. Remember, what you resist, persists!

Don't conflate adrenaline sensations with anxiety. They're not the same thing, although those suffering with anxiety often define them as such. And this error is a huge precursor to the development of an anxiety disorder! Where else could consistently and erroneously judging your bodily sensations as bad or dangerous lead to but anxiety? And potential panic!

There are countless examples demonstrating that adrenaline and anxiety are not one and the same. Here are a handful of examples of adrenalized experiences, sans anxiety:

* The adrenaline rush felt by a roller coaster lover at the top of the freefall

* A bride's adrenalized excitement on her wedding day

* An MMA fighter blasting heavy metal to increase energy and aggression

* A surfer's adrenaline high while surfing a tube

* The thrill of going out on a first date with someone you find super attractive

If adrenaline was equivalent to anxiety, then adrenaline junkies wouldn't have so much fun engaging in death-defying activities like skydiving, base jumping, free climbing, river rafting, and eating peanut butter sandwiches without jelly (just making sure you're still with me here!). In the book *Heroic Efforts*, Jennifer Lois reported that search and rescue volunteers have been shown to interpret their adrenaline rushes as not only exciting, but pleasurable.[1] Adrenaline junkies love the exhilaration of it all.

Consider astronauts. Astronauts have long been thought of as almost a different breed of human—free of typical anxiety and so brave. The truth is, though most of us would consider flying to the moon a brave act, if you aren't afraid, you can't be brave. Courage requires fear to label an act courageous. Were Buzz Aldrin and Neil Armstrong afraid? You can bet that when they were the first to step onto the moon in 1969, adrenaline was flowing. Still, it seems they've never characterized this as an "anxious" experience, even with the uncertainty of what they would encounter on this strange terrain. In a recent interview, Buzz Aldrin mentioned being completely focused on the mission.[2] You can bet adrenaline, in part, was supplying that focus! If Neil Armstrong was anxious, he might have said something like, "Get me off this crazy boulder. I miss Earth. Mommy!" when first stepping onto the moon. Instead, he made the famous remark, "That's one small step for man, one giant leap for mankind" (Though just a tip, Neil. Next time say "humankind"!).

Always remind yourself that adrenaline can be triggered by many experiences other than fear, such as an unfamiliar situation. The brain's determination that the body requires energy or focus (like when in competition) can start up when engaged in any activity you find exciting or exhilarating, or when feeling overwhelmed, uncertain or, yes, afraid.

The experience of non-fear-based adrenaline can be described by many names, such as "being in the zone," "good anxiety," and "eustress." Some of these names suggest that there are positive stressors, such as the aforementioned roller coaster ride or playing well in a tennis match. Other names and associations suggest adrenaline can be a motivator, pushing you to do your best, when so desired.

Nevertheless, all names for the experience of adrenaline without fear speak to my point. And that is, if you experience adrenaline and there is nothing you fear in that moment, then it is not anxiety!

And what does this non-anxiety-based adrenaline do? The same things that all adrenaline does. It increases energy, expands lung airways, maximizes concentration, improves reflexes, enhances tolerance to pain, quickens heart beat to propel more blood to the muscles to make you stronger, tightens vision, and more.

By the way, when you're overwhelmed or uncertain and that triggers adrenaline, it does not necessitate anxiety, either. When a single woman is on a date she's excited about, there might be a lot of uncertainty. Will the date go well? Will this be the person she falls in love with? Will she get spinach stuck in her teeth? Dating breeds uncertainty. This doesn't mean one is *afraid* while dating, even when adrenaline is the third wheel. It's interesting to note that, although uncertainty doesn't equal anxiety, those that struggle with anxiety do struggle with uncertainty, too (also known as a lack of control).

With regard to feeling overwhelmed, the same applies. For example, you might secretly date several people at the same time and be overwhelmed. This does not suggest, however, that you're experiencing anxiety. In fact, though overwhelming, juggling multiple dating opportunities might be something you enjoy. Of course, for others this might lead to spontaneous anxious combustion over fear of calling someone by the wrong name. But it is an error to equate anxiety with feeling overwhelmed. You can be overwhelmed and not anxious. Anxiety is always about fear. The experience of being overwhelmed usually means you have a lot on your plate. Fear is not required for that reality.

Anxiety or Adrenaline?

When disturbed by adrenaline in any given situation, to ascertain if you're experiencing anxiety or just plain old adrenaline, ask yourself: What do I fear right now? If unsure, question all the possibilities. Be introspective and honest. If you fear nothing at the moment, then you know it's not anxiety. It's just your system picking up on your brain's stimulation of adrenaline, based on one or more of these variables:

1. You're in a situation where your system requires energy, effort, or intense focus.

2. You're overwhelmed or entering a situation marred with uncertainty.

3. You're engaged in an exciting or exhilarating activity.

Determining that there is no fear in an adrenalized moment can be a twofold accomplishment when it comes to your anxiety getaway! First, it assists you in accepting your neurobiology and the realities of adrenaline's functions. And, even more importantly, it can be a preventative measure against your brain reinforcing, fueling, or promoting false fear messages!

EXPOSURE IS YOUR ANXIETY BULLDOZER

"If you are falling...dive."

—Joseph Campbell

"Just do it."

—Nike

You've made it to the master strategy for outsmarting your brain's false fear messages. And—exciting news—it's *scientifically proven* to help you overcome fear! Remember, there is no anxiety without fear. Anxiety *is* fear. This chapter on exposure and the next on modifying your false beliefs are the keys to unlocking the door to your anxiety getaway. When these two are done in conjunction, there is no more powerful anxiety treatment (or scientifically proven one at that!). So, a little figurative drumroll please, because...

It's exposure time!

A BIT MORE BRAIN STUFF

Do you remember my train track analogy from chapter 3 addressing your brain's neuroplasticity? To jog your memory, neuroplasticity is defined as the brain's ability to change its neurochemistry. So just as our brains can be taught fear, they also have the capacity to unlearn fear. You can change your brain's response to your anxiety-provoking stimuli by creating new neural pathways or, as my analogy states, laying down new brain train tracks. And guess what? Exposure is the track that can take your anxiety train to bye-bye land!

In the scientific community, the consensus based on several studies is that symptoms of anxiety are primarily attributed to a piece of brain called the amygdala. Remember the amygdala? It produces emotional responses, including fear and the establishment of fear-based memories.[1] The amygdalas of those with anxiety disorders have consistently been demonstrated by neuroimaging as disturbingly hyperactive during fear responses.[2] This means that with the mistaken interpretation of a threat, your little amygdala can be erroneously triggered. And if the false labeling of a threat is followed by your avoidance, well...say hello to the creation of your enemy. I'm talking about false fear messages!

The hyper-activation of the amygdala during an anxious episode can literally be seen with positron emission tomography, known more commonly as PET scans. But as proof and a great source of inspiration, so can the results of exposure. Many PET scan images can be found online of the anxious brain both before and after exposure.

For example, you can find images demonstrating the activation of the amygdala with spider-phobic subjects before and after exposure treatment.[3] The pre-photo shows anxiety getting busy! The post-photo following exposure clearly shows the extinguishing of this anxiety. No more spider fears!

Not only do PET scan images demonstrate the proven effectiveness of exposure, but they also attest to the brain's neuroplasticity. Everyone's brain has the capacity to change its neurochemistry. Or, as mentioned earlier, to create a new neural pathway toward the extinction of your fear. And fortunately, we've got Cognitive-Behavioral Therapy with its scientifically proven strategy of exposure at our disposal! Are you ready to lay down those new brain train tracks? I hope so, because when you're done with this chapter, you'll feel like a train conductor in charge of sending your anxiety locomotive to splitsville.

Quick and Dirty Exposure Definition

Exposure is a scientifically proven Cognitive-Behavioral Therapy (CBT) strategy defined by facing your fears, whether external or internal, in a systematic (usually gradual) manner. Exposure is conducted with the goal of adapting or desensitizing your brain to your anxiety-provoking thought, image, impulse, or situation. The classic name for exposure is "Exposure and Response Prevention." Response prevention simply means deliberately facing one's fear without engaging in avoidance.

GET USED TO IT

For the purpose of making your anxiety getaway, we're going to focus on one of the many amazing things our brains have the capacity to do, if proper steps are taken. I'm talking about our brain's ability to adapt. It is this ability that is such a wonderful gift when it comes to overcoming fear and claiming your calm. The truth is, unless strong fear is involved, our brains often adapt through exposure without our awareness *if* we place ourselves in situations over and over and over again. For instance, our brains adapt to new jobs, new homes, new neighborhoods, new dogs, new cats, new haircuts, and so on.

One of my favorite examples (and one I share with patients in my office almost every work day) is a print of a colorful turtle above my desk. I placed it there the day I moved in, a number of years ago. I still recall enjoying it every day—for only two weeks. For those turtle-focused two weeks, I'd walk into my office, take a look, and say to myself, "That turtle looks so good there. I love turtles. And what a perfect spot I found for that print!" But alas, after two weeks, I don't know if I ever really *saw* that turtle again. Sorry, turtle. Don't get me wrong, I still like the print and its location. My brain just adapted to its presence. The print became part of my office wall. Of course, if that print was in a different spot every time I arrived at my office, other than thinking someone was gaslighting me, my brain would not adapt to it being on that specific wall above my desk. My brain adapted because it's what brains do, but only if you feed them proper, consistent stimuli.

Think about the items in your home. Maybe a print on the wall? Maybe some trinkets around the house? Just consider something that's been there a while, something that remains in one place. Now, unless you interact with it every day, is it really something you notice regularly? I assume not. That's because your brain has adapted to it and its placement. Again, this is what brains do. And this is what your brain can do with your fear. Exposure enables your brain to adapt, so that you and your brain can be unafraid!

Generally speaking, like most things in life, there are pros and cons to our brains adapting. ER interns adapt to the victims of accidents and violence that enter the emergency room screaming bloody murder night after night. Surgeons, after a given number of the same surgery, begin to see patients more like body parts. And people who consistently choose addicts or batterers as romantic partners have adapted to that experience, perhaps so much so that they find some sort of comfort in its familiarity.

But when it comes to tackling anxiety through exposure, there are no cons! The fact that our brains can adapt to fear is the key to overcoming it! Your brain can adapt to fear, so that it can stop itself from sending false fear messages and no longer be afraid. And exposure is the scientifically proven method to outsmart your brain's false fear messages and achieve this adaptation.

There are many words used to describe this adaptation in the field of psychology. One is habituation. Another is desensitization. They all mean the same thing. Our brains can get used to anxiety-provoking events and thoughts to the point that they no longer stimulate our former anxiety or discomfort.

Our brains can even get used to some of the things we actually enjoy (or did enjoy, anyway). For instance, I intellectually know that the Eagles' "Hotel California" is a monumental rock song (I'd rank it in the top ten, for sure). But, I'm no longer interested in hearing it ever again! I've heard it probably a thousand times! Okay, slight exaggeration (though not by much). When the acoustic version was shared, it was interesting and brought me some joy, once again. But now, I've heard *that* about a thousand times, too! At this point, whenever "Hotel California" pops up, I change the channel. And no current "Hotel California" fan is gonna stop me! I have no anger about it. I just now find it boooring. A big old snoozefest! You see, my brain has adapted to it. My brain no longer finds it interesting. It no longer brings me joy. And though I might occasionally miss my "Hotel California" joy (a bit dramatic for effect), this is a shining example of the goal of exposure. It results in pure, unadulterated boredom.

HEY, ANXIETY! YOU BORE ME!

Boredom with what makes you anxious is the true goal of exposure. It's not to never be anxious again (good grammar!). That's probably not possible. We live in an uncertain world and we're all human. But, if your goal *is* to never be anxious again, you're resisting anxiety—the very experience that creates it! For example, it's not a reasonable, healthy goal to never have a panic attack again because this means you're still afraid, which will encourage more of them! It's that old battle again. Exposure is about removing the battle, so your brain adapts and you're not afraid any longer.

You can't be bored and anxious at the same time. Neurologically speaking, if the brain becomes desensitized to fear-based stimuli, there is no fear. And that is your goal: to overcome anxiety, so it doesn't cause suffering and create a limitation. Your goal is to stop anxiety from interfering with your life, or from being a barrier of any kind. But to fully achieve this goal, you must achieve brain boredom. So the goal of exposure is not really anxiety reduction, it's really boredom. Anxiety reduction is just a byproduct.

Another way to think of the boredom you can achieve with exposure is as indifference. Indifference means you simply don't care. No love or hate, not really even like or dislike. You just don't give one iota. This is what exposure ultimately achieves. Exposure can generate indifference to your fear, so you just don't care and then it's no longer there for you to beware.

An easy example of indifference that often springs to my mind is baseball (if you love it, I apologize). I know it's considered the national pastime, but it just does nothing for me. I don't like it or dislike it. I just don't care about it. The World Series could be on TV and I might not know it. If I ever go to a game, I'll enjoy the experience, but not because of the game itself. I'm focused on the food and the fans, not the game. Baseball doesn't affect me in any way. I just don't care.

This is the goal of exposure! To simply not care about your fear. But whether you call the result of exposure boredom or indifference, this is what it can achieve for your brain...and you!

SEXY EXPOSURE STORIES FOR YOUR READING PLEASURE

Okay, so maybe they're not *sexy*. But via the following analogies, stories, and examples, I'm going to clarify what exposure is all about. Let's start with an analogy I use in my office frequently when treating patients.

Aikido

Ever heard of it? Aikido is a very unique martial art. Its difference lies in its focus on using the attacker's force against them. So for example, if your attacker is pushing you, instead of pushing back (the natural inclination), an aikido move might be for you to pull. The attacker's momentum is already heading in that direction anyway, and if you were to pull and step aside, you could send the attacker flying! Check out some Aikido master YouTube videos and you'll see what I mean! Aikido is a perfect analogy for what exposure is all about. In exposure, we use the momentum of your fear by going with it, welcoming it. Exposure is counterintuitive. Your false fear messages encourage you to run away. With exposure, you run right at them (though in small, easier sprints, so to speak). Again, exposure is the opposite of what you're inclined to do in the face of fear, which is...face it! Recall the quote by Joseph Campbell that I mentioned at the beginning of the chapter. "If you are falling...dive!" That is the definition of exposure! As has been established in the prior chapters, if you avoid anxiety, it will follow you like an angry bee. And then bzzzzz—you're stung! Your assignment to overcome your fear is, figuratively speaking, to head for the beehive! But don't fret. This can be accomplished in small, gradual doses. Perhaps one bee at a time.

Swimming Pools

A common metaphor for exposure that's been bandied about by anxiety treatment specialists for years is that of a cold pool. When people conjure up memories of cold pools (especially in childhood), most seem to know what happens if you remain in the water for about fifteen minutes. Whenever I ask my patients if they remember what happens, they answer knowingly, "You get used to it." And they are, of course, correct. You get used to the water. You're not more comfortable after fifteen minutes because the temperature of the water has grown warmer. The temperature is the same as when you first entered—still very cold. It's just that your body has adapted. You've acclimated. This is analogous to exposure for anxiety. Just like getting used to a cold pool, you must stay *in* anxiety to get used to it. If done properly, this is what our brains do. But what would happen if you ran up to the cold water, stuck a toe in, quickly pulled your foot away and ran back to the comfort of your lounge chair? If you said "You would never get used to the water"... Ding, ding, ding! You win the prize! And it's the same for anxiety and exposure. You've got to stay in it to win it.

Here are some examples of real-life (*in vivo*) anxiety exposures you can plunge into, to overcome your fear:

* Remain in a specific environment for a specific amount of time. For example, if you fear hospitals, go sit in a hospital lobby.

* Stare at a photo for a specific time. For those afraid of needles, stare at a photo of a phlebotomist ready to draw blood.

* Engage in an activity you fear for a specific time. For example, if dancing in front of people makes you anxious, dance for one song at a club.

* Interact with something you fear for a specific time. If you fear birds, then hold a parakeet at a pet store for a bit.

* Share a symptom you fear when out in the world. For example, if you fear sweating, splash water on your forehead, then go take a stroll out in public for a while.

Bad Tasting Medicine

A heads up: You're going to feel anxious while engaging in exposure! How could you not? You can't expect to face fear and feel comfortable. That just wouldn't make sense. If that were possible, there wouldn't be any fear at all, for anybody. When you feel anxiety during any level of exposure, you're doing it absolutely right! This is what's needed to stop those false fear messages. When you find that you're anxious during exposure, it means you're on the path toward your anxiety getaway. You've found the proper exposure. Your anxiety is a good thing, and you need this anxiety. How can your brain adapt if you're not feeding it what it needs to do so? If you don't feel anxious during exposure (before your brain adapts, that is), then the exposure you're doing is not exposure at all.

Think of exposure as bad tasting medicine. Do you remember ever having cough syrup as a kid? Well, I hated it. I found it disgusting, even though it often helped my cough. Exposure is just like that. It's bad tasting medicine! It's not fun, but it's not meant to be. Still, you might find that over time, the act of facing your fears becomes invigorating and empowering! Believe it or not, it happens.

Unfortunately, I'm sorry to say that your anxiety with exposure can get worse before it gets better. Sort of like a sinus infection. But why would that be? Because now, rather than avoiding fear, you're purposely placing yourself in anxiety-provoking situations—perhaps both mentally and physically. Think about it this way: if you feared lions, you couldn't reasonably expect to be less anxious the deeper you crept into a lion's den. You'd be more anxious! But, there is a silver lining to this short-lived increase in anxiety. This increase in anxiety is an indicator that you're even closer to extinguishing it. Bad tasting medicine, remember?

With proper exposure strategy and structure, purposely facing fearful stimuli until anxiety decreases is how the brain adapts. You can call it adaptation, habituation, desensitization, or liberation. You can also just focus on achieving the true goal of boredom or indifference. Any way you slice it, with successful exposure, the salient point is that your brain no longer experiences your former fear as anxiety-provoking.

For skeptics or those horrified over the thought of doing any exposure at all (often one and the same), I typically begin with a special assignment, one unrelated to their fear to prove their brains can adapt just like everybody else's. On that note, if you're skeptical or resistant, try the following exposure I assigned Nadine (with your own object modifications, as needed).

Nadine's Special Assignment

Almost from the moment she entered my office, Nadine shared her intense concern over facing any of her fears at any level. Dubious, but still hopeful, she discussed having tried so many different anxiety treatment methods over the years that she had little faith exposure would work. After all, nothing else had before. I explained that faith isn't required for progress with this evidence-based approach, and that Cognitive-Behavioral Therapy with exposure is scientifically proven to be effective.

To help Nadine transcend her doubts by proving the effectiveness of exposure, I gave her two simultaneous, non-confrontational assignments. I had her wear her bracelet on her other wrist for two weeks and move her wall calendar in her office to another wall. Though at first uncomfortable, she adapted to both in seven days. That's exposure! And, as mentioned earlier, we experience it all the time. We're often just not aware of it. We adapt to a new hair style, a new classroom, a new piece of furniture at home, a new romantic partner's idiosyncrasies, new glasses, a new car, a new boss, a new job, new coworkers, being a parent, fear of panic attacks, unrealistic thoughts of going broke, a needle phobia, and so on. It's all exposure if you do what's necessary for the brain to become desensitized. Again, you don't have to *believe* exposure works to experience its effects, though it's a far more inspiring and less reluctant process when you do!

STOP THE CLOCK AND START THE COUNT

There aren't just time-oriented exposures. You can also practice frequency-oriented exposures, especially when you have a straightforward fear that demands a simple, straightforward assignment. For instance, when I work with anxious children, they often fear images seen in film trailers, TV commercials, and on billboards (usually of the horror movie variety). Most of us remember certain fear-inducing images that brought us sleepless nights as children. And some of us, though we've been adults for a long while, still have the faces of these movie monsters tattooed on our brains. Some of us take it a step further, thinking of them every now and again when alone and the house creaks at night. Luckily for these anxious kids, a straightforward frequency exposure can work quickly, if they're willing to try.

Mia, age 13, was terrified of the Annabelle doll from the popular horror movies. When I treated her at the time, there were constant TV trailers and ads that showed this doll committing multiple acts of violence. One billboard in particular presented Annabelle peering over the shoulder of a child while she was sleeping. Mia had barely slept for three weeks, often running into her parents' bed nightly for comfort. Of course, this only served to maintain her fear through avoidance. To Mia's credit, she was highly motivated to overcome this fear, not only due to the suffering it was causing, but also due to the embarrassment she felt running to her parents' bed at age thirteen. I prescribed Mia the exposure assignment of watching the Annabelle trailer online thirty times over the course of one week. That did the trick! Mia reported a week later that she was back in her own room all night, completely comfortable and with no fear of Annabelle pulling that seriously creepy, peering-over-the-shoulder bedtime ploy! Mia's brain had adapted to the image and moved on. It was as if it had been neurologically erased. It was now boring!

Anxiety Getaway Tip

For those of you with kids who struggle with this class of fears, the above exposure is exactly what you should have them engage in. Maybe add a prior, agreed-upon reward for facing their fear, too. Motivation is key for all, when it comes to facing fear!

Below are more frequency-based exposures. Review them to determine if they're a good match for your anxiety:

* Read an anxiety-provoking article a specific number of times each day or week. For example, if a parent is struggling with an obsessive fear of their child being kidnapped, I'll often assign them articles about kidnappings. What else? No one said exposure was fun! As usual, I instruct them to seek an article that initially triggers their anxiety to a three on the anxiety scale. They then focus on re-reading that same article until their anxiety reaches a one or zero consistently, before moving on to the next, ever more anxiety-heightening article.

* Watch a fear-inducing YouTube video a specific number of times each day or week. For those who fear public speaking, the video might be of an embarrassing incident for a speaker.

* Write down a trigger word or phrase directly related to your fear on a slip of paper. Then carry it around in your pocket or purse and look at it twenty times a day. For example, for those with fears about heart trouble, the phrase might be "massive heart attack."

* Listen to a song that provides a reminder of your fear a certain number of times per day. For those with sweating fears, James Brown's "Cold Sweat" can work wonders after fifty listens! Plus, as an added bonus, you'll bring in the funk! And believe it or not, there are many other songs from other artists focused on sweating. Though for some reason, none mention deodorant for that other kind of funk. But I digress... Just find a song that matches your particular fear!

* Repeat a word or phrase related to your fear a certain number of times per day. For example, for those with a fear of making a mistake at work, they can repeat the phrase, "Oh no, I'm going to make a huge error at the office today." Probably best to only say this out loud at home, though!

IF YOU'RE WILLING TO THINK IT, YOU CAN OVERCOME IT

Sometimes, real-life exposure opportunities aren't going to be available to you, or there will be limitations on exposure. Exposing yourself to fear of flying is a perfect example. Unless you're independently wealthy or your work forces you to travel, you probably can't get on a plane a few times a week for exposure purposes. So what do you do? Give up? Hell no! This is when you turn to your imagination.

As described in chapter 3, the brain often doesn't know the difference between what is real and what is imagined. So thankfully, for our purposes, you can turn to your imagination to expose yourself to your anxiety.

"Imaginal Exposure" has many uses. For instance, it can be used as a gradual step on the way to real-life exposure. For those with PTSD, it can be used as "exposure" to fears based on traumatic memories. Further still, imaginal exposure can be used when your anxiety is focused on events that have never happened—those classic "What If" thoughts.

Emily came to me with a fear of losing her mind. An obsession, really (we'll talk about these in the OCD chapter, too). Since recently seeing a schizophrenic man on the street, she was terrified she would "turn crazy."

Like many fears that require exposure led by imagination, there will be some real-life exposures to be done, as well. For example, Emily could watch movies or YouTube videos featuring "crazy" people. She could read articles about schizophrenia, too. But what she couldn't do is expose herself to actually losing her mind. So, she had to practice imaginal exposure.

HOW IMAGINAL EXPOSURE IS DONE

The most straightforward imaginal exposure strategy is to write a story of your worst fear realized. A story where the experience you're most terrified of happening, actually happens. Sounds fun, doesn't it? Remember, bad tasting medicine.

Here are your writing instructions:

1. Write your worst fear realized story as if it is actually happening right now—first-person, present tense.

2. Don't include anything in the story that's soothing. Don't allude to how your anxiety has decreased or is manageable. Include nothing to make yourself feel better. Allow yourself to cry, if needed. (Sorry, but it happens. It can be part of the process.)

3. Start your story where your anxiety generally begins. What is your trigger? Include anticipatory anxiety, too. This is defined as anxiety that comes in anticipation of an upcoming event. Or it's simply anxiety about having anxiety!

4. Make your story more vivid by describing all five senses during the experience of anxiety. In other words, if possible, write what you see, hear, smell, taste, and touch. This will bring it to life, so it takes you deeper into the exposure, adding to its strength. Keep in mind, it doesn't have to be a well-written story. Just be specific and do your best to describe your experience.

5. Your story doesn't have to be lengthy. A half- to a full-page is fine, as long as it covers your anxiety experience completely.

6. Focus your story on your anxiety building to a crescendo. Describe how it's growing worse, along with increased consequences.

7. End your story with your worst fear coming true. Many stories end in death (or some derivative thereof). Yours may or may not.

8. When finished writing your story, your exposure assignment is to read it a certain number of times per day. You can also record it on a voice recording app and listen to it a number of times per day. Either way is fine. As you read or listen, remove all distractions. Focus on the exposure. Allow your story to pull you into the experience of your anxiety.

9. Continue this exposure assignment until your story no longer triggers anxiety.

Emily's Imaginal Exposure Story (a.k.a. Emily Loses Her Marbles)

"I'm getting ready for work in the morning. I'm putting on my make up in the mirror and I think I see something behind me. I jump and turn around. There is nothing there. I must have been hallucinating. What if I'm going crazy? What if I'm losing my mind? I finish putting on my makeup. I feel super nervous. Jittery. I make breakfast. A spinach smoothie with some fruit as usual, but it doesn't taste the same. It tastes weird to me. I check the date on the spinach and it's still fresh. And it looks fine. Maybe I'm losing my taste buds? That's probably something that happens to crazy people. I put the smoothie down because I'm too anxious to drink it. When I put it on the counter, I hear a noise from the other room.

"I go check, but there's nothing there. I think I might be hearing things. I really must be starting to lose my mind. Stressed about getting to work on time, I try to ignore this and leave. I get in my car. I drive my regular path. The world seems a bit fuzzy. It feels different. Oddly quiet. I feel strange. I'm losing it. I think about those hallucinations at home. I'm starting to feel weird and different. Really strange. This must be what crazy people go through when they first lose their mind. I feel dizzy. And nauseous. By the time I get to my office, I'm an anxious wreck. I sit down at my desk and try to get some work done. I can't focus. I can't concentrate. It feels like people are staring at me. Like they notice something's wrong with me. Like they notice I'm starting to lose my grip on reality. My friend Kelly looks at me strangely. She must be thinking the same. What am I going to do? My boss is going to see this and fire me. I head to our regular weekly meeting with the whole company. And now I'm really nervous because I feel like something is going to happen.

"In the middle of the meeting, I lose impulse control and make a strange face. A grimacing face. My colleagues notice and stare. My boss asks me if I'm okay. I spit out, "Yes, I'm fine." But I'm not! I try to carry on, but my eyes start rolling back-and-forth, back-and-forth. I'm sure I look so insane! I'm freaking out. I'm becoming a schizophrenic. Becoming psychotic. I suddenly start babbling incoherently. Like I'm speaking in tongues. My colleagues and boss don't know what to do. Then I start screaming aggressively. Yelling about nothing or no one in particular. I get up from my chair and then fall down. I start writhing on the floor, like I'm possessed. I hear someone scream, "Call 911!" The psychiatric team gets there within two minutes. They immediately determine that I'm crazy. They put me in a straitjacket and haul me into their truck. They take me to the mental hospital where a doctor determines easily that I'm schizophrenic and psychotic. They take me away and put me in an isolation room with foam on the walls. I scream, dance, and laugh inappropriately. I'm told I have a visitor. It's my husband. My work must have called him. He tries talking to me, but I can't interpret his words. I've lost my mind completely. He looks heartbroken and shakes his head. Then he walks away with a sad wave. I've now lost my husband and my job. My life is over. I'm a mental case. And that's it. I accomplish nothing else in my life. And I just sit there staring at the walls. With all the other locked up crazies. For years."

In addition to your imaginal exposure story, there is another imaginal exposure strategy you can add, if applicable to your fear. It's called...acting. I'm sure you've heard of it. You don't have to be a serious actor to use this strategy, but you do have to bring the drama! It's easy. Here's how it's done:

Just play pretend. Pretend that your worst fear is happening right now. In addition to instructing Emily to write her story, I encouraged her to act insane when alone at home! So for a set time a few days a week, Emily would bark, twitch, yell out, and pretend to hear or see things. This additional exposure, along with her story, was essential to her brain's adaptation. She put in the work and received the reward. Soon, she was no longer afraid that she was losing her mind.

Imaginal exposure is powerful stuff. Use it as much as possible. Use it when you have a fear that is difficult or impossible to confront in reality. Use it when you have an anxious thought you can't shake. And use it as an add-on to real-life exposures. All anxiety is ultimately thought-based, so it makes perfect sense that you may need to use your imagination to confront it! To move beyond anxious thoughts, welcome them. Purposely think about them and use your imagination to take them to a ridiculous level—all the time! I know it's unpleasant, but you've got to turn the tables on your anxiety. You have to go with it. No resistance. No battle.

This is exposure and you're seeking brain adaptation, so demand that your anxiety "bring it on!" This is the warrior attitude that you must adopt, so your brain can adapt! Take your thoughts to their furthest extreme.

If you have contamination fears (a classic OCD obsession) and you're afraid of unexpected contact with fecal matter (that's right, I'm talking poop!), imagine yourself covered in it. Imagine yourself in a room filled with it. It's rising, engulfing you. You're swimming in it—a pool filled with poop.

If you have a fear of your plane crashing when en route, don't just imagine a lackluster crash. Imagine one hundred ear piercing screams and the plane going down in flames, lighting up the sky. If you remove all resistance to your thoughts, your anxiety has nowhere to go.

Pleasant thoughts, these are not (unintentional Yoda phrasing). But if you purposely encourage these anxious thoughts, you'll turn the tables on anxiety. And if you put in the exposure time, your brain will be on the road to responding with boredom! Again, take your anxious thoughts to the extreme. No resistance. Your brain will soon adapt and the false fear messages will soon end.

Anxiety Getaway Tip

Keep in mind that if you have an external fear, you can't only face it with imaginal exposure. To overcome it, you'll have to face it in reality, too. For although the brain has trouble distinguishing between what is real and what is imagined, imaginal exposure won't be enough. Why? Because if you don't face your fear in real-life (when possible), it means that you're avoiding it. And what does avoidance do for anxiety?

Exactly! It encourages, reinforces, and maintains it. A golden rule of exposure is that if you can expose yourself to your fear in the real world, do so. Make these real-life exposures your foundation because you'll be encountering them in your real life. If you don't face these fearful situations, how will you make your anxiety getaway? In addition to real-life exposures, you can engage in imaginal exposure for gradual help along the way to conquering your biggest fear. The more exposure the better.

"BUT, I'VE BEEN PRACTICING EXPOSURE FOR A WHILE"

After being taught exposure, some of my patients respond with, "Well, if that's exposure, I've already been doing it. So why am I still totally anxious?" It's a good question. Here's the answer:

It's not exposure if you're white-knuckling it, just trying to survive. For example, I've consistently treated people terrified of flying who, prior to our work together, still boarded their flights. And during those flights, they did all they could to battle their anxiety. They took Ativan or Xanax, or bought alcohol, or just held onto their seat for dear life the entire flight, desperately hoping to make it to their destination in one piece. These are not the same as exposure. Sure, a case could be made that a small degree of exposure is achieved just by getting on the plane. And that can't be discounted. Obviously, to overcome fear of flying, you're going to have to board that plane, so it's a necessary, big step. However, if you're fighting anxiety by just trying to survive, it's not effective exposure. Exposure must be deliberate. Remember, fighting anxiety encourages, reinforces, and maintains your anxiety (yes, I'm saying it again because you need to own this). It's that battle that I described in the earlier chapters. It is resistance. And the brain knows the difference. It knows the difference between whether you're fighting anxiety or welcoming it.

If you welcome anxiety by purposely facing it, your brain will soon have a different response. Figuratively, it will say "Wait a second, Bob (feel free to insert your name here, unless Bob works for ya!). You've been afraid of this terrible danger and I've tried to protect you, but now you're purposely welcoming this horror by deliberately facing it? Something's going on. Why am I sending you fear messages if you're letting me know there's no need? I might have to amend that!" Well said, Bob's brain!

So fighting anxiety in any capacity is not a true or helpful exposure. You've got to welcome it. Exposure is about purposely inviting anxiety, exposing yourself to your anxiety deliberately.

Misumi, another former patient, was terrified of dogs and knew most people wouldn't understand, so she was thankful she'd been able to hide her fear for several years behind a false pretense of allergies. That is, she did until her boss acquired a schnauzer and brought it to the office!

Misumi loved her job and was good at it. In fact, there was an opportunity for advancement and she knew she was at the top of the list. She certainly didn't want her anxiety to impact her negatively at work now. And she wanted her boss to focus on her work alone, not her fear. Misumi needed help fast, as that schnauzer was about to become an office fixture. She arrived in my office full of dread, but desperate to overcome her anxiety right away! After expressing her willingness to face intense fear and possible panic immediately, we chose "flooding" and devised her exposure plan. Flooding is an exposure technique that entails facing one's worst fear first and directly, with no gradual approach. Misumi's key assignment was straightforward: I sent her to a dog shelter and instructed her to interact with all kinds of dogs. Her nightmare! But, like a fear-facing warrior, she visited that shelter every day for a week, staying several hours at a time. And then...she was no longer afraid. By the end of that week, Misumi was taking several dogs on walks—and enjoying it! To this day, she has no problem with her boss' schnauzer or any other dog with whom she crosses paths, though as a matter of preference, she remains a cat person. Hey, I'm not in the business of changing personalities!

I rarely see people willing to endure the challenge of flooding. The obvious benefit is that it offers quick progress. The obvious downside is that it can be downright terrifying for most. Thankfully, it's not necessary. Exposure is equally effective at a slow and steady pace, as long as you're consistent. So go at your own pace. This is what 90 percent of my patients choose. Returning to the cold pool example, if you immerse yourself full tilt by jumping in ("cannonball!"), you'll get used to the water more quickly. That's flooding. You're facing the worst of it first. If you wade in to your ankles, then your knees, and then your waist, it'll take longer. That's gradual exposure. But, the end result is the same. You'll be used to the water, just like the cannonballer. The time of the achievement does not matter.

SEVENTEEN HOURS

Over the years, my work with anxious patients has shown that it takes an average of about seventeen hours (not all at once!) for the brain to adapt to a level of fear via exposure. Just consider it the amount of time you're awake on any given day. You might need a little less, you might need a little more. But ultimately, it's got to be around seventeen hours of facing your worst fear realized. Prior to that, you potentially need seventeen hours of exposure to every fear trigger on your list before facing your worst fear realized—unless you choose seventeen hours of flooding, like Misumi. But you can't face a minor fear for a total of seventeen hours, adapt, and then expect that to result in overcoming your largest fear. That doesn't make sense. Your exposure progress doesn't work up. However, it does work down. **For instance,** Misumi's seventeen hours of exposure facing her largest fear of interacting with dogs made it a piece of cake to observe a dog on a walk with its owner around the neighborhood. However, if Misumi began with gradual exposure instead of flooding, by only observing dogs on walks, the result would be different. It would simply resolve her fear of seeing a dog on a walk. It wouldn't resolve her fear of interacting with dogs! But observing a dog on a walk could be the first step on the way there. See what I mean?

LET'S TALK "EXPOSURE STEPS"

Exposure is all about looking fear in the face and welcoming it—which soon sends it packing. It's counterintuitive. If you follow these basic exposure steps, you'll be on your way to your anxiety getaway:

1. **Identify your fear:** Think about your anxiety. Ask, "What am I afraid of in the realm of this fear?" Consider all of it. One of the keys in doing proper exposure work is knowing exactly what you fear. This can take

some effort. In fact, sometimes we make assumptions about what frightens us, when it might be something else. If you do this with exposure, you might take yourself in the wrong direction and waste time! So figure out what *really* makes you anxious.

2. **Make a list:** Make a comprehensive list of everything that triggers your particular anxiety. From the minor related fears to the major ones. Stay on topic, though. If you have multiple fears, you'll have to make multiple lists. Your fear list could include thoughts, situations, places, images, objects, other people (including family members), words, memories, movies, TV programs (like the news), and songs. Yes, it's going to take some work! Don't most worthwhile things?

It's important to be clear about what you ultimately fear. The fear that terrifies you to your core. The fear that, should you overcome it, you'll no longer be afraid! That's what you're after.

Keep in mind, lots of exposures can help as you work your way toward your biggest fear. But it's most beneficial to find exposures that trigger your fear on different levels. Once you begin exposure, you'll start with small fear triggers that don't take you into absolute terror. This is gradual exposure. You'll take it step by step. On your list, be sure to include different levels of fear—even in the same environment or situation, if applicable. For example, if you fear peanut butter, eating a big spoonful would be a high anxiety rating exposure. However, sniffing an open jar would be much lower. Staring at an open jar would be lower still. Staring at an open jar from across the room, even lower.

Anxiety Getaway Tip

Each exposure assignment must trigger anxiety from the start. As you make progress on the assignment, it will decrease. If there's no discomfort from the start, then the assignment is too easy or it's incongruent with your fear. There's nothing to adapt to without anxiety or discomfort. An exposure that does not cause anxiety is no exposure at all. It's a waste of time. You need anxiety to get over anxiety! You must seek it out. Remember, bad tasting medicine.

3. **Assign a rating:** Once your fear list is replete with many levels of your fear, assign an anxiety number rating to each. Do this by considering how much anxiety you believe each will trigger on an anxiety scale of zero to ten (zero signifying no anxiety and ten signifying a head-popping-off level of anxiety). Once you confront each level, you can make an adjustment if you find you have less or more anxiety. Remember, you're going to start off slow and build. I know at this point it can be hard to believe, but you will eventually be able to face your biggest fear. You can and you will, if you commit.

Living in New York City, Sally never feared bees, though she saw them from time to time. When she first moved to Los Angeles, bees were the last thing on her mind—until she went on her first hike up one of LA's many hillsides. Hiking with a friend one morning, she soon saw a commotion. Moving closer, she saw hikers slowly surrounding a young woman in pain. She had been stung by a bee. In that moment, Sally became hyperaware of the fact that she had never been stung. Her mind raced with thoughts of bee stings and anaphylactic shock. Her friend suggested they keep walking. But what if other bees were waiting further up the trail? Sally's mind ran wild. So, much to the chagrin of her friend, Sally hightailed it out of there, back to the trail entrance and to the safety of her car.

Right then and there, Sally said "adios" to hiking altogether. When friends invited her for hikes after that, she made up excuses of prior plans. But that's not all—she started avoiding parks. Parks contain bees. And she avoided walks where there were lots of trees and flowers. Soon, when forced to be around a lawn, shrubbery, or any nature at all, she felt panicked. Her heart raced and she felt dizzy. She started avoiding these areas completely, too.

Carrying on, she tried to convince herself that all was fine with her now small life in Los Angeles. And it was, until she met her partner who loved to hike—and Sally's partner wanted her to share in the experience! Sally knew this was a great idea because exercising with your partner can be a great way to connect, talk, and share. Plus, Sally wanted to lose some weight and enjoy the Southern California sun while doing so! And introspectively, Sally knew her anxiety was irrational. So she decided she'd have to give hiking another shot soon. But what about...the bees? Sally was terrified and didn't believe she could defeat her fear. She arrived in my office with trepidation, but ready to work. So we began. Check out the fear list Sally completed at home after our first session.

Sally's Bee Fear Exposure List

(In no particular order. Later re-arranged by anxiety rating for ease of following a gradual exposure plan.)

* Watch bee videos on YouTube:
  * A teenager finding a beehive in his backyard (4);
  * A man covered in bees (5);
  * Bees found in a park (6).
* Listen to bee buzzing sounds (7) while walking outside (10).
* Go to the zoo to see the bee exhibit (5).
* Read articles about bees found on hiking trails or in backyards (5), and articles about bee stings (8).
* Walk in the park (9).
* Walk near trees and bushes (6).
* Walk on the beach (6).
* Go on a hike (10).
* Hang out in a hiking trail parking lot (8).
* Look at photos of bees online (3).
* Write down the word "bee" and carry it in purse (3).
* Watch movies featuring bees (3).
* Write a worst fear realized story (Imaginal Exposure) and regularly read it (8).
* Drive by nature or a hiking trail (1).
* Carry fake, but realistic, toy bees in purse (7).

4. **Choose your assignment:** After assigning your anxiety ratings, it's time to choose your first exposure assignment. Start with a fear trigger on your list that causes you about a three on the scale of anxiety. A three is often a level that many can handle. It's a good, usually tolerable, place to jump in and get started. You've been afraid for long enough. Why waste more time? If that sounds too terrifying, find an assignment that will take you to a two on the anxiety scale. You're going to face this anxiety triggering item over and over again, until you're no longer afraid. It's best to start with what *you* can handle. Sally started with looking at photos of bees, especially bees found on trails and hillsides.

Anxiety Getaway Tip

During the exposure, do nothing but face your fear trigger. Do not try to calm yourself with deep breathing or distraction methods, like chatting on the phone or listening to music. That would be like going into a cold pool with a wetsuit—you can't get used to the water that way, though it tricks you into believing you are. Using calming or distraction methods during an exposure is an escape. It's avoidant. Remember, to overcome fear you've got to remove the battle. This is the point of exposure. You're turning the tables on your anxiety. If your brain had its own voice separate from you (false fear messages suggest it already sort of does), it might say during exposure, "What are you doing? Don't you know this could kill us? This is crazy!" However, with consistent exposure over time, your brain will say, "You're trying to tell me something. I thought this was supposed to be dangerous. I guess you're telling me it's not. Okay, got it!" And then you can claim your calm.

5. **Decide on length:** Once you've chosen your first exposure from your list, you must decide on the initial length of your exposure assignment. Fifteen minutes is a good start. Some research has shown that the longer the exposure, the better. Forty-five minutes has been a common standard for the ideal exposure length. That said, you've got a life, so you can plan your exposure lengths within reason as long as you're making progress.

Remember, you get out what you put in. This is true for every endeavor in life. With exposure, your hard work and dedication will pay off in claiming your calm. Won't that be worth it? Put the time in and reap the rewards, but find some balance. Live your life while doing your exposure work consistently, but also consider how long you want to be dealing with your fear and its treatment.

On your way to seventeen hours, if you want to get over your anxiety triggers in a speedier fashion, it's best to do a lot of exposure in shorter periods of time. For instance, those of you who were athletes in high school or college might recall "hell week." Hell week was often conducted at the beginning of the season or in preparation for it. It usually consisted of two practices a day, or very lengthy practices with a great degree of intensity. Most athletes will remember it as hellish, but rewarding. Looking back, it was questionable (even then) whether or not it was a healthy practice. Putting that much strain on one's joints in such a short period of time may not be advisable for one's future. And this is where my sports analogy ends when it comes to exposure. Because when it comes to anxiety exposure, the more the better! If you're willing and able to devote two weeks of your life to as much exposure as humanly possible, you'll make much quicker gains! You could create your own personal hell week, times two! You could engage in three or four hours of exposure per day! If you compare two weeks of hell to how long you've been struggling with a particular fear, it won't seem so long. You could reasonably overcome a large amount of your fear in this period of time, or at the very least make incredible gains!

Still, unless you're in a hurry and willing, two weeks of hell are not necessary. Let's go back to the cold pool example for a moment. As mentioned, there are some people who run and jump in. They're the cannonballers. They get used to the water more quickly because they've immersed themselves in it—an intense exposure all at once. Then there are those we'll call the dippers. They slowly enter the water, just a little dip at a time. Maybe they begin with water up to their waist and stand there for a while. They might splash some water on their shoulders. Then they slowly crouch down until the water laps at their neck and stay there for a bit. And then, finally, comes the face dunk! It might take a while to get used to the water in this manner. However, when contemplating the dipper and the cannonballer, at the end of the day you've got two people equally used to the cold pool temp. All of this to say: you choose your own length and intensity of exposure. There is no race! In time, you'll face all the fear triggers on your list. You set your own pace. It's up to you. If you want to get over your fear more quickly, you'll put more exposure time in toward reaching seventeen hours for each fear trigger (if needed). Or you'll face your largest fears right out of the gate. If you're not in a hurry or you're too terrified, then move more gradually from lower anxiety triggers to higher ones.

6. **Rate your level twice:** Once your exposure work on a particular anxiety trigger from your list is underway, be sure to rate your anxiety level at the beginning and end of every exposure session. Again, rate your anxiety on a scale from zero to ten. Ideally, you want your anxiety at the end to be half of what you rated it at the beginning of your session. To reduce your anxiety by half may require a longer exposure (potentially forty-five minutes or more). That said, as long as it has decreased by even one scale point, you're on the right path! Like "The Tortoise and The Hare," slow and steady can win the race, so just keep doing your exposure.

Remember, as an average standard, it takes about seventeen hours of exposure for your brain to adapt to a specific fear. That might seem like a lot, but keep a proper perspective. In total, that's not even a full day for a fear that's been plaguing you for much longer! You might be pleasantly surprised to find that the smaller fears on your list only require a few hours of exposure in total before adaptation occurs.

As a reminder, you can't adapt to a smaller fear and expect your brain to adapt to larger fears. Each exposure is focused on your brain adapting to that particular fear trigger. For example, if you have a fear of public speaking, after facing an audience of ten people for a total of seventeen hours and adapting, you can't expect to easily face an audience of a hundred. Exposure works down, not up. This means that if you face a larger fear, some of your smaller fears can fall away. But you can't expect to face a smaller fear and have your larger fears fall away. That's just not rational. Overcoming the fear of speaking to an audience of ten means you'll now be comfortable with audiences of ten or less. On the plus side, as you continue to work your way up to your biggest fear (perhaps speaking at a company event) with gradual exposure, you'll be adapting to speaking to audiences in general—along with adapting to other public speaking variables like the microphone, being on stage, the lights, and more. And these gains will make speaking to growing audiences more tolerable. So it might take another seventeen hours of exposure to overcome anxiety around an audience of twenty, and then thirty, and so on. But you won't be starting at an anxiety level that may have been intolerable to you before. With each exposure success, as you gradually move up your list of higher intensity fears, each larger fear beyond the last will be more tolerable. In other words, fears you initially rated at a seven may now be at a five on the anxiety scale, following your brain's adaptation to other earlier fear triggers.

Anxiety Getaway Tip

The average seventeen hours of exposure do not need to be consecutive. No need to perform seventeen hours of exposure in a row—in one day! As long as you're consistently engaging in exposure on your way to an average of seventeen hours, you're doing it properly. Just don't leave more than three days between exposures. Consider your exposure work like going to the gym or being on a diet. You can't leave too many days between gym or dieting sessions, lest your bad avoidance habits lead to inaction. You've got to be consistent to see results! Similarly, you've got to be consistent with your exposure to see results with your anxiety. To stay on track, be sure to log your exposure time in a notebook or diary, or on your smartphone.

7. **Decide when to move on:** When engaged in an ongoing exposure assignment, continue to rate your anxiety. Once your anxiety consistently rates at a zero or one on the anxiety scale at the end of each session, it's time to move on to the next fear trigger on your list. You've extinguished that particular anxiety trigger!

I know number scale ratings can sometimes be a challenge to determine. As a guideline, a one rating is negligible, meaning you might not know whether the slight discomfort you feel is tension, stress, or simply adrenaline. Don't move on to the next fear trigger on your list before you rate each fear trigger at a zero or a one. Finish out the assignment. Be patient. Do the work! Build the foundation so your brain can adapt and you can outsmart those false fear messages.

8. **Don't end too soon:** If you find you're equally as anxious at the end of your exposure sessions as compared to when you began, you might be ending when your anxiety is still at its peak. When Sally began exposure for her fear of hanging out in hiking trail parking lots, she realized that

fifteen minutes weren't cutting it anymore. At the end of her fifteen minute exposure sessions, her anxiety was repeatedly at the same rating as when she began—an eight on the anxiety scale! Although fifteen minutes had been an appropriate exposure length for smaller assignments (like looking at bee photos online), this wasn't the case for this more challenging exposure. She needed to increase the length of her sessions.

Remember, to help your brain adapt to your fears, you've got to stay in each exposure session until your anxiety has decreased by at least one point on the anxiety scale as compared to its rating when you began. This is the indicator of progress, and this is why paying attention to the anxiety scale during an exposure session is important. After increasing her parking lot exposure to twenty-five minutes, Sally noticed her anxiety decreased from an eight to a five by the end of each session.

If you cut out of an exposure while your anxiety is still at its peak, you're unintentionally re-teaching your brain that the only way to handle this fear is to run! And, as I've said enough times to annoy you (*excusez-moi!*), running from anxiety encourages, reinforces, and maintains it. So if you're not making progress on an exposure, but you're aware that it still triggers anxiety, then it's simply not long enough. Extend your exposure session by ten minutes and see where that takes you. If your anxiety is still not budging much, extend it further. Your anxiety might require a lengthier exposure session before experiencing any decrease. If you need more time, do more time!

Anxiety Getaway Tip

Another reason you might still be anxious, even after a total of seventeen exposure hours, is that you might not have determined the proper exposure. In other words, the fear trigger on your list might not speak to the true source of your anxiety. The exposure must trigger the actual fear you're focusing on extinguishing. Sometimes, getting to the heart of what you fear with exposure requires some adjustments.

9. **Do mini-exposures:** If you want to make quicker progress, in addition to your main exposure assignment of the moment, do a lot of mini-exposures to deluge your brain with the same fear-based stimuli. These mini-exposures will be less challenging (a lower anxiety-provoking level than your current exposure) and should not require much more time. Think of them as exposure boosters. In addition to your current main exposure assignment, you are to practice mini-exposures throughout the day to consistently immerse your brain in fearful stimuli. Remember, we're trying to push your brain to adapt to your anxiety. The more exposure the better! So surround yourself with your fear!! Inundate your brain!

Here are some exposure booster examples:

*   Tape photos of your fear (or its reminders) on your fridge, walls, and bathroom mirror—any place you frequent—so you'll see the images often.

*   Carry around a piece of paper with a word that sparks your fear.

*   Listen to songs in the car that remind you of your fear.

*   Do the smartphone exposure below!

Smartphone Exposure

Set a specific image, word or phrase as your smartphone wallpaper. How many times do you check your phone on a daily basis? If you're like most, it could be fifty times or more—a great mini-exposure opportunity, and a low effort one at that.

Laura was worried she was blinking too much. In fact, she couldn't get blinking off her mind. This is what you'd call an obsession. To cope with her blinking anxiety, Laura tried to stop herself from blinking too much. This, of course, backfired and caused her to blink a lot! When you try to control an involuntary bodily response, you wind up interfering with its natural automatic process. So, in an effort to curb what she feared was excessive, Laura's blinking became unnatural. This then triggered more anxiety and a greater increase in her attempts to stop thinking about blinking. Remember, whatever you resist persists. Laura needed to learn that to stop thinking about anything, you've got to think about it a lot! So as a mini-exposure, I had Laura write the term "blink" on a slip of paper, take a photo of it, and set it as her smartphone wallpaper. Thus, every time she glanced at her phone, she saw the word "blink." This was a great added exposure to her primary assignment of blinking often on purpose, while at home watching TV, eating, and reading (these were five-second exposures spaced out frequently, so as not to injure her eyeball muscles!). Eventually, her brain adapted to the fear-based thought of blinking too much. The thought became boring. Her brain became desensitized. No more fear!

10. **Set a precedent:** Follow my precedent rule of exposure: once you act on a particular exposure and accomplish it, you do not go backwards. This exposure becomes your new baseline. Over the years, I've had many patients decide on a given day to challenge themselves with much more fear than their current exposure. This has usually coincided with a day when they felt strong and rested. So on this given day, they chose to jump a few levels on their fear list and face a greater fear. Fantastic! An excellent and courageous act! I would never discourage them from facing more of their anxiety. And I won't discourage you. But...

A frequent occurrence has been that a day or two later, for a variety of reasons, they haven't felt as strong as that fateful day. It might be due to work stress, or exhaustion, or a foul mood. It could be anything. Whatever the reason, on that day, they just don't feel quite up to facing that heightened level of fear again. Rather than face more anxiety, they return to an earlier exposure level or don't do any exposure at all. What's wrong with that? Well...

They've just re-taught their brain that the only way to handle fear is to run. By avoiding the exposure they faced when feeling strong, they've now, once more, reinforced their fear—the very process they're working to change! That's why it's important to know what you fear and work toward it gradually. The danger is that if you face a higher degree of fear too quickly, there might be days that follow when you just don't feel up to the task. There are going to be good days and bad days in the process of treating your anxiety. Do your best to choose an exposure that is achievable now and on days where you might feel less than stellar.

I must repeat: I'll never discourage you from facing fear. If you want to go for it, then go for it! Face a big level of fear that you haven't faced before. You can do it! Way to go! I'm cheering you on. But know that once you do, that must become your new starting point for more exposure. After all, by accomplishing a new level of exposure on a given day, you've just proven that you can do it! Why go backward? Going backward reinforces your fear neurologically by firing up the neural pathway responsible for sending those same old false fear messages—the very process you're trying to undo. One lesson I'm sure is becoming crystal clear is that this treatment cannot support avoidance. It supports facing fear in a measured, structured way. So once you establish a precedent of what you can do when it comes to your fear, that is your new baseline! For if you achieved it once, you've proven you can achieve it again. On good days, on bad days, on any in between—you can clearly do this. That's your new starting line. That's the precedent rule!

Anxiety Getaway Tip

There will be ups and downs on the exposure road. It's not easy facing fear. If it was, no one would have any. So never beat yourself up over setbacks. It

CHAPTER 5: EXPOSURE IS YOUR ANXIETY BULLDOZER

won't help. And you're only human—if you happen to make an error by ignoring the precedent rule, that's okay. What's done is done. Just return to your prior exposure assignment and stay until your anxiety rating is consistently at a zero or one. Then you can move on to greater levels of fear!

11. **Go one at a time:** If you have multiple unrelated fears and you've got the time, you can do separate exposures simultaneously. Just create a fear list for each. However, that approach can be overwhelming for most people. Unless you're prepared to face multiple fears at once, it's best to prioritize. Start with one fear. Once you've overcome that one, then work on facing the next. The best way to prioritize is to determine which fear is causing you the most suffering right now. Start with that one first! Get to the others later.

EXPOSURE CLOSURE

You can't fight symptoms inside the way you fight problems outside. Battling internal struggles, like anxiety, requires a different kind of fighting technique. We've been indoctrinated to this notion of taking the fight to the enemy by beating them into submission. But you can't fight your anxiety this way. Remember my Aikido analogy? You have to welcome anxiety to beat it. You have to invite it in. You must say, "Do your worst, anxiety! Bring it on!" Exposure is a counterintuitive approach. It requires the opposite action of what you're inclined to choose—which is to run. Remember, we are biologically set up to seek pleasure and avoid pain (a.k.a. discomfort). Exposure is about seeking anxiety's discomfort.

Here's something to reflect on if you're still reluctant to face your fear, even in the gradual manner I've shared. You've got two choices: You can choose short-term discomfort followed by long-term calm, or you can choose short-term calm (a.k.a. avoidance) followed by long-term discomfort.

Exposure is where it's at. It is *the* scientifically proven strategy that changes your brain's neurochemistry by extinguishing your anxiety. No breathing exercises, no hypnosis, no acupuncture, no amount of exploring your unresolved childhood conflicts or anxiety's "root causes," and no amount of positive thinking will be effective in overcoming an established anxiety disorder. Exposure is the key. There is no way of truly overcoming fear without it.

I know some of you who read this might try to skirt exposure anyway, and I get it. Exposure is no day at the beach. It's unpleasant, and maybe you're not tired enough of the limitations anxiety has placed on your life. Maybe you're not ready mentally to take exposure on. But if not now, when? Anxiety struggles don't get easier the longer you have them, but maybe you've found a way to live with anxiety's barriers. Maybe you believe you're too afraid to face them and you're hoping to feel more confident in the near future.

Confidence is earned. It doesn't just appear someday, detached from action, though some wish for this very experience. You earn confidence by doing. Confidence is a byproduct of action, and exposure *is* action—the action that can stop those false fear messages in their tracks and help you make your anxiety getaway.

Now some of you might be tired of your anxiety, but decide to keep looking for a quick, easy, no-effort, no-fear fix—a magic bullet. Be warned: if you do this, you'll waste time and money while continuing to be in pain. If you want to defeat anxiety, you'll be back to the necessity of exposure soon enough. So why not do it now? Most people, at some point, realize that life goes by in the blink of an eye. Talk to anyone in their eighties and they'll tell you so. This life is yours to live, or not. It's up to you. I know exposure is scary. All of my patients for over twenty years have been scared, too. But those willing to do the work I'm prescribing in this book will experience progress every time. You get out what you put in, like most things in life. If my patients can do it, you can, too! So roll those sleeves up and jump in. The water might be cold at first, but you'll get used to it! You can do this. You can stay in the water, though your lips might be turning blue, until you're used to it.

Remember, your anxiety isn't a weakness. It's not about you, really. It's about your brain promoting false fear messages based on your unintentional encouragement. But you can teach your brain to develop a new response to what you fear. You can outsmart these false fear messages and claim your calm by following the steps in this chapter. Just go at your own pace, but be sure to push yourself. Don't be lazy. Commit and be consistent. Your confidence will grow as your brain adapts to each new level of your fear. You'll start to feel empowered. And who knows? You might even experience what some fear-facing warriors describe when they're in the thick of it. Exhilaration! Yep, it's possible. All it requires is one step at a time.

In the coming chapters, we'll focus on the specific anxiety issues of panic attacks, phobias, and OCD. These are where you'll most likely find your diagnostic category of anxiety and learn even more specific techniques to help yourself.

But first, we must talk about the other essential strategy—one that, when combined with exposure, creates a powerhouse that can solidify your anxiety getaway for years to come. It's about your false beliefs. Once you're equipped with the skills to modify them, you'll combine both major strategies into a powerful one-two punch to anxiety's face and claim more long-lasting calm! So let's get to it!

CHAPTER 6

STOP BELIEVIN'

"A widespread belief is more often likely to be foolish than sensible."

—Bertrand Russell

"The sleep of reason produces monsters."

—Francisco Goya

"Highly illogical."

—Spock

Society practices so many false beliefs, it's no wonder we're often unaware of the spell we're under that removes our calm and creates anxiety en masse. We are consistently inundated with messages that support our false beliefs in the form of our community, our state, our country, public figures, entertainment, employment, media driven ads, and last but certainly not least, communication with our family members and friends. The messages are sweeping and seem limitless, but include, "There are just winners and losers," "The rich are happier," "Marriage is about kids," "Those with the most exciting Instagram posts lead the most exciting, care-free lives," "celebrities are special people," and "the car you drive symbolizes your worth." There are hundreds more that we create all by ourselves (more anxiety-specific ones are described soon in this chapter)! It's no wonder that every year, in the United States alone, there are approximately forty million people suffering from diagnosable anxiety.[1]

WHAT'S A FALSE BELIEF?

But what is a false belief? The answer is easy if you take it logically (Paul Simon lyrical reference for you readers aged forty and up!). Stating the obvious, it's a belief that is not true, or one that's not fact- or reality-based. For further clarification, there are countless examples, an easy one being a child's fear of the dark. What child hasn't thought, at one time or another, that the shape staring at them with the lights off is a hungry monster in the mood for a midnight snack? However, once the lights are on, the monster is revealed to be a chair. The false belief, of course, is that there's a monster in the room. The reality-based belief is that there is no evidence of monsters and this child was falsely reacting to sheer chair terror.

For the purpose of helping you claim your calm, it's important you understand that in actuality, there is only one reality. Not *your* reality or *my* reality. Contrary to what many believe, you do not create your own reality. The more accurate statement would be that you create your own *illusion*. There are not multiple realities, just one factual reality. You do, however, construct your experience of life based on the beliefs you hold. This would make your experiences feel real to you, whether they're based in reality or not. Beliefs have consequences and, generally speaking, most anxiety symptoms are a consequence of false beliefs.

FALSE BELIEFS DON'T NEGATE, THEY CREATE

So how do beliefs specifically create anxiety? In chapter 3, you learned of the amygdala's role in the creation of anxiety. As a reminder, the amygdala is responsible for the formulation of fear and the establishment of fear-based memories, once it receives a danger message—correct or not. You may recall, as discussed in earlier chapters, that your brain can establish fear solely based on messaging. And barring grief, love, real life-threatening events, and maybe a few other transcendent emotional experiences, belief creates our emotions. So, the materialization of fear and the creation of that fear memory usually begins with what one believes about an event.

Take a moment right now to think about your personal anxiety issue. Consider the most basic belief of danger that sustains it. For example, to trigger anxiety, those with a fear of clowns (yep, it's a real fear called "coulrophobia") would have to believe that clowns are dangerous to their well-being in some way. But if your anxiety trigger can't do you any harm in reality (like clowns), then this is the first indicator that you've set your anxiety in motion based on a mistruth! Even when you have a fear that could be dangerous if it came to fruition, your anxiety is, most likely, based on a *current* mistruth. Like with fear of heights—it's only dangerous if you're actually falling or at a real risk of doing so! And these may just be examples of an elementary fear associated with your anxiety. A deeper dive is usually necessary to correct what may be a bucket full of other associated false beliefs (instructions on how to do so follow soon!).

Moving forward, I suppose you have to ask yourself whether you want to believe that which is true or that which is false. I hope it's the former. Few people say they want to believe in what is false. Why, then, are false beliefs so prevalent? Because we are unaware of our false beliefs until we realize...they're false. And I'll admit, sometimes false beliefs have their appeal, especially in the form of fantasies.

Let's face it, fantasies are fun because it's nice to focus on what makes us feel good. For example, sometimes it's nice to dream of absolute power and royalty. But fantasy is an illusion and, sooner or later, that fantasy bubble is going to burst because it's not real. The bigger the attachment to fantasy, the bigger the probable burst.

Some false beliefs make you feel better for far longer than a fantasy, but reality eventually arrives and results in you feeling worse. Much worse. For example, for many in their twenties, believing they've got all the time in the world to pursue a goal might be okay. But what about those in their fifties, sixties, and seventies? At a certain point, you've got to take action. Otherwise, life will dispel the false belief of infinite time by giving you a big ball of regret over wasted opportunity with a newfound physical decline. Bummer!

And though you might be unaware, what if your false beliefs don't make you feel any better at all? Not even for the moment that fantasies or other false beliefs provide? For example, what if you believe nobody is to be trusted? Intense suspicion of everyone will not lead to many close relationships. In fact, it's going to keep you far away from any real closeness or intimacy with anyone. Maintaining this false belief will most likely result in ceaseless loneliness with a wall around your heart that you never allow to crumble. Pretty bleak, wouldn't you say?

So how, then, are false beliefs helpful in any way? Especially when they generate anxiety? Here's the answer: *They're not!*

The challenge with false beliefs is they often exist on a deeper cognitive level, muddying the waters of awareness—at least until you bring them to the surface. Whether currently aware or not, if you struggle with anxiety, you can bet you're practicing false beliefs that only serve to encourage it.

To be crystal clear, false beliefs are detrimental to your calm because they create, encourage, reinforce, and maintain anxiety. Even with the proven effectiveness of exposure in extinguishing false fear messages, if false beliefs are maintained, they'll keep your anxiety fire lit. Not only will they undo the exposure progress you've made, but they'll continue to promote anxiety. All this to say: *false beliefs bad* (nothing like a little Frankenstein speak for emphasis)!

I recall working with Hannah, a meek married woman in her thirties, who was terrified to ask for her needs to be met. It wasn't that her husband was inconsiderate.

In fact, she contacted me after being prompted by her frustrated husband, who was imploring her to work on this struggle. Hannah had never been one to ask for what she needed—she felt anxious just considering doing so. Needs she ignored included both major and minor, such as asking her husband to turn down the TV while she was reading, stating her opinion on what movie to see on a weekend night, reminding her husband to ask before making plans as a couple with friends, and requesting to be kissed while making love. We began working with exposure to face Hannah's fear of asking for needs to be met, while we simultaneously explored her attached false beliefs.

Hannah did well with exposure. At first, she was terrified to ask her husband for what she needed or preferred. For example, she always found it daunting to respond with a preference when her husband asked where she'd like to have lunch. Her typical response was, "I don't care. Wherever you want." Via exposure, Hannah quickly adapted to this anxiety trigger and others. Gradually, she adapted to asking for much larger needs that previously triggered an even greater degree of anxiety. Hannah was surprised to find her husband was happy with her progress! He shared relief that he no longer had to fish for what Hannah preferred in their day-to-day lives. And more importantly, Hannah felt less anxious asking for what she needed, following her great progress with exposure. However...

Hannah soon started to backslide. Even though she had faced a large amount of fear, she still had a longstanding false belief that asking others for what you need was selfish, petty, and a nuisance to people. We examined this false belief in earnest.

I should state that with exposure progress alone, initially Hannah's perspective had somewhat changed. Not only did her brain adapt to fear, but she realized that her husband was welcoming, not angry, when she voiced her needs. This is an example of a long-held tenet of Cognitive-Behavioral Therapy, which basically states that if you change your behavior, your thinking can follow. But this is a rare occurrence if you have entrenched false beliefs—those that have been around for a long while and permeated many aspects of your life. Those false beliefs tend to require some heavy modification. This was ultimately the case with Hannah.

As you might imagine, our beliefs—true or false—have an undeniable effect on our lives. But for our purposes, what's most important to understand is that false beliefs are almost always responsible for anxiety! How you might ask? Let me count the ways...

There are three central ways in which false beliefs create anxiety:

1. **They inform our choices**. This means that false beliefs have a profound impact on both the path we follow and how we treat ourselves and others. For instance, if you believe that following your passion in life is immature and irresponsible, you'll probably make choices based only on paying bills and doing what is expected of you. You'll consistently be anxious about engaging in your interests, if you make the attempt to face this discomfort at all.

2. **They impact how we experience the world**. This means that false beliefs have a huge impact on how we feel and respond. For example, if you believe that people always lie and cheat, you'll feel anxious over the prospect of counting on others.

You might even lie and cheat to keep the score even. You'll have trouble building close relationships, not allowing yourself to be vulnerable due to anxiety over others potentially taking advantage. Why would you be vulnerable if no one is trustworthy? Plus, without trust, you won't generate loyalty. If you believe people have a devious agenda, you won't have others' best interests at heart—sort of a requirement to build loyalty! Can you see how this false belief alone generates anxiety and can touch so many aspects of life?

3. **They directly create anxiety**. Choices and experience notwithstanding, there are false beliefs that create anxiety straightaway. For instance, if you believe wrinkles mean death, then wrinkles will probably result in anxiety!

These three ways in which beliefs manifest anxiety are not mutually exclusive. They often operate in unison to create and propagate fear. For example, if you have a fear of the dentist, you probably believe that all dental work is flat out painful. How could anxiety not result from a belief like that? But in addition to this false belief directly linking to anxiety, it could inform a choice to avoid dental work, while practicing another false belief that all dentists are barbaric. For instance, someone with a fear of the dentist might believe that dentists are heartless human beings who enjoy inflicting pain on innocent patients. This belief would only encourage anxiousness toward dentists and their work, and with continued dentist avoidance, eventual tooth loss!

Back to Hannah and her false belief that asking for what she needed was selfish, petty, and a nuisance.

Hannah was indoctrinated early on by her family into false beliefs about "a woman's place." And although she intellectually knew many of her beliefs were born of sexist ideology, they had been modeled and taught to her since she was a child. Simply put, they were well baked in. When it comes to belief, most of us are products of our environment, until we choose a different path and modify false beliefs! This was certainly the case for Hannah. Although she made initial progress with exposure in extinguishing her false fear messages, it was short-lived. Her false beliefs quickly unraveled her gains.

Despite my attempts, Hannah was resistant to facing the falsity of believing it was selfish, petty, and a nuisance to ask for her needs to be met both in her marriage and other relationships. With each attempt during our work together, Hannah defended her false belief with super commitment. And when she was unable to find another unproven explanation for its validity, she attributed it to her upbringing. She was unwilling to even imagine it was a sign of a healthy relationship to assert one's needs in marriage, and to sometimes even consider herself first.

We went around and around for a while. Soon enough, Hannah stopped asking for what she needed in her marriage altogether. When I pointed out that she was again ignoring her needs, Hannah remarked that she just didn't see the value in considering them. My suggestion that she was not teaching her kids the importance of self-care and assertion fell on deaf ears. When I asked if her husband was frustrated with the return of her prior behaviors, she acknowledged that he was and added that he was giving up. In fact, she reported him saying that if this return to former behavior reflected a lack of desire to change, she should discontinue her anxiety treatment. She did just that two sessions later. Anxiety treatment is rarely successful if entered just to please others.

The impact our belief systems have on our lives cannot be ignored, and when it comes to anxiety, our beliefs are almost entirely responsible. Subscribing to false beliefs that encourage anxiety is a little like starting a fire and throwing gasoline on it. Thankfully, exposure can be done to undo your brain's self-created false fear messages. But, as seen above with Hannah, exposure is not enough if you continue to feed false beliefs. So false beliefs alone often generate anxiety, but they also serve to erode the exposure gains you make—a false belief double whammy. This is why it's essential to modify your false beliefs!

● ● ● ● ● ●

Nara's experience is another good example of the three ways false beliefs create anxiety and permeate one's life. Nara contacted me for help with "lots of worries." These included worries about acing her college exams, a long-running tendency to re-read passages to confirm she was comprehending them, and a frequent concern about leaving her phone behind. Causing further anxiety, she took three times as long as others to complete her assignments. If that wasn't enough, Nara was also overly apologetic if or when she felt she "messed up."

During our initial discussion, it quickly became clear that Nara had an intense fear of making mistakes! At some point in life, she adopted false beliefs that making mistakes always led to "bad things happening" and that they diminished your worth as a person. To Nara, mistakes somehow meant that she was less than. Nara committed to changing these false beliefs as they led not only to time wasted, but also to intense anxious suffering!

The reality is we are all fallible beings. We make mistakes, but mistakes are part of learning! Perhaps it would be best to call them *errors*. Doesn't the term "error" seem less loaded and judgmental than "mistake"? The truth is, no matter what you call them, we will continue to make them until we learn. All errors offer this opportunity. That's a fact. And even then, there is no failure. To call something, someone, or yourself a failure over an error is a judgment and false belief. For instance, Thomas Edison made thousands of unsuccessful attempts to invent the light bulb. During that time, he reportedly said, "I have not failed, I've just found 10,000 ways that won't work."

Nara worked hard at exposure—she stopped herself from re-reading passages, checked only once for her phone, decreased her apologies, and even purposefully made mistakes on homework assignments. But she also put the required effort into modifying her false beliefs, and soon saw great success! She was no longer panic-stricken over the prospect of making a mistake and even believed that it was okay to make them from time to time. Nara maintained her progress, understanding fully that it was essential to change the false beliefs that created her anxiety in the first place. For if she still believed it wasn't okay to make mistakes, she would create the same anxiety problem all over again, thus spinning her wheels.

BELIEF AND FEAR: PARTNERS IN CRIME

False beliefs are the common theme throughout all anxiety struggles. Let's for a moment consider a fear of elevators. Unless an elevator has detached from its cable and is plummeting to the bottom floor toward a bone-crushing, fiery crash, the survival instinct's fight-or-flight response is likely being triggered without any real danger. Say hello again to false fear messages. And where did they originate from? You've got it! A false belief.

There can be no fear without belief. How could there be? To be afraid, you must believe that something is harmful to you in some way! If you believed elevators were a thrilling, joyful ride or, at the very least, no threat to your well-being, there would be no fear. To be anxious over elevator rides, one would have to believe a ride on the elevator will lead to a harmful negative, such as kill them, encourage them to lose control, force them to empty their bladder, trap them, stop them from breathing, or whatever other anxiety-inducing false belief the mind can cook up!

So to claim your calm, it's essential to modify your false beliefs by replacing them with reality-based beliefs. The long-range goal is to adopt reality-based beliefs as your new perspective, which influence how you interpret danger, interact with the world, and experience life itself.

When done in conjunction with exposure, the combination is unbeatable! Living a life where you extinguish false fear messages with exposure, and false beliefs with reality-based thinking is imperative for a life filled with freedom from anxiety. It's how you make your anxiety getaway!

Once you've overcome whatever fear had you in its grip, consistently shifting your perspective toward believing what is true is the most effective way to continue to encourage calm. As you may be starting to imagine, when it comes to anxiety (and life), the benefits of reality-based thinking are many.

BENEFITS OF THE REALITY WAKE-UP CALL

Below is a list of the benefits of adopting reality-based beliefs. Once you start practicing more reality and fewer falsehoods, you'll experience more and more of these advantages:

* Less anxiety/more calm
* More solution-focused problem-solving
* Increased conflict resolution
* Greater self-control
* More confidence
* Feeling of empowerment
* Heightened ability to judge threats properly
* More respect from others
* Greater achievement
* Freedom from self-imposed barriers
* Enhanced awareness
* Less stress
* Less worry
* Accelerated hair growth (Not the case. Just wanted to make sure you were still paying attention to these amazing benefits!)

FALSE BELIEFS OF ANXIETY SUFFERERS AROUND THE WORLD

Below are some common, basic false beliefs I've observed for over twenty years. Each false belief is accompanied by reality-based beliefs with which to counter them. Do you hold any of these general anxiety-producing or anxiety-maintaining false beliefs? Read them all and apply them to yourself. Better still, start practicing the reality-based beliefs that accompany them. Here you go:

* **False Belief:** Anxiety is the worst.

* **Reality-Based Belief:** What makes anxiety *the worst*? Especially considering that, for the most part, you're creating it and are in charge of resolving it. Isn't it great that it's in your power to rid yourself of anxiety? And isn't it great that it can't kill you, and that it's only debilitating if you allow it to be? You can't say that about so many human struggles, such as cancer, Parkinson's disease, multiple sclerosis...the list goes on.

To feed the false belief that anxiety is the worst also encourages your victimization. You are not a victim of anxiety if you're the one creating it. And if you created it, you can undo it. Follow the steps in this book and make your anxiety getaway!

* **False Belief:** I can't take it.

* **Reality-Based Belief:** You're reading this book. That simple fact shows you can take it! Why? Because here you sit. You're still here! You haven't spontaneously combusted. And I assume there are other things you do in life that demonstrate you can take it, too. You might not like anxiety. You might want something better. If that's the

case, then you'll do what's required to change your circumstances. That's why you're reading this book. And I agree, anxiety stinks! But you certainly can take it!

* **False Belief:** Anxiety is a sign that I'm a weak person.

* **Reality-Based Belief:** Where is your proof that anxiety means you are a weak person? Reality demonstrates that human beings have all sorts of struggles. As has been established, you've unintentionally taught your brain to fear your current anxiety trigger. Your brain is now responding erroneously with false fear messages. It's what the brain does. It's got nothing to do with you being weak.

Millions of people struggle with anxiety. Some don't share it with others and instead fear in hiding, stuck in an anxious prison. Others pretend they're not anxious and cope with anxiety through drinking or drug addiction. Others still find different ways to cope— some healthy, some not. But you're in the company of millions. Clearly, anxiety is a human issue. And you're a human, so...why not you, too?

The reality is, the more you work on your anxiety and make progress, the stronger you'll feel. Either way, anxiety does not mean you're a weak person. Even if you decide to ignore the steps in this book and accept anxiety as your lot in life, that decision would not make you a weak person. In reality, it would point to you as a person who is allowing fear to consume them and inform their choices. It would point to you, perhaps, as being stubborn and unwilling to try to change your life. It would point to you as someone who is accepting this limitation. Obviously, it would point to you as someone maintaining false beliefs. So all of those would be true, psychologically and behaviorally speaking. Still, anxiety doesn't mean you're weak.

* **False Belief:** Anxiety is shameful.

* **Reality-Based Belief:** What makes anxiety shameful? You're a human being and most human beings have some kind of struggle. Maybe anxiety has been yours? Again, everybody's got something. Take a look around at your friends, family, or even just strangers on the street. One person struggles with depression, another with a weight problem, another with dating, another with alcohol abuse, another with diabetes, and yet another with chronic loneliness. Everybody has something.

It's true, our society has promoted shame by way of a stigma against mental health issues. But if you take a moment to consider it, there is a constant cascade of false beliefs perpetuated by our society and culture. Promoting shame for those with anxiety is just another. And just because loads of people believe something certainly doesn't make it true! For example, millions of people believe in the concept of "jinxing" oneself. As in, "It's going well, but let's not talk about it because I don't want to jinx it!" This, of course, has no basis in reality. How could it? We're not that powerful, though some of you jinx believers will fight me tooth and nail on this. Despite how it might feel sometimes, the universe is not conspiring against us in reality. It's not saying, "Hey, I'm responsible for things going well for you, and that's fine. But if you talk about it, I'll ruin you!" And yet millions of people believe in the power to jinx.

If those who judge you over your struggle with anxiety were to take a look at their own false beliefs, they'd likely find many that are equally unreasonable. Anxiety is simply an issue to work on resolving. And in this way, it's not dissimilar to a multitude of other issues. Thankfully, it's something you can change! Be proud of the fact that you're reading this book, preparing to take the steps necessary to claim your calm. That's courageous. That's admirable. That's inspiring. There's nothing shameful about changing your life!

* **False Belief:** I'll always be anxious. I don't see how I can overcome this.

* **Reality-Based Belief:** When it comes to our choices, most circumstances don't change unless we actively work on changing them! Anxiety is the same. The cognitive-behavioral techniques in this book have been scientifically proven to work. They've helped too many people to count. What makes you so different that they can't help you, too? You're human, aren't you? Just like everyone else—but in your own unique and special way, of course!

Listen, I know it's sometimes difficult to see the light at the end of the tunnel. Sometimes we don't know how we can possibly change. And we can't see around corners. In those moments of doubt, all you can do is stay on the proven path outlined here. Just focus on taking step after step. Clichés abound regarding this reality. "Journey of a thousand miles..." and such. Or baby steps. On and on. As NHL hall-of-famer Wayne Gretzky said, "You miss 100 percent of the shots you don't take." You'll always be anxious if you don't do what's required to change. If you continue to avoid facing your fear (here I go again), you'll only encourage it, reinforce it, and maintain it. So you've got to put in the effort, and then it will change. However, if you practice the defeatist false belief that you'll always be anxious, it might inform your choice to avoid doing anything about it. That would be sad. But it's all up to you! And that's the truth.

* **False Belief:** No one else seems to have the anxiety I struggle with.

* **Reality-Based Belief:** Millions of people every year struggle with diagnosable anxiety. This alone suggests that there are many people who struggle with the exact same kind of anxiety you do. So although you might be unique and special in your own unique and special way, your anxiety is not. It's just plain old anxiety that's highly treatable (by the methods I've given you in this book!). The false belief that your anxiety is somehow different instills and encourages a victim mentality. The truth is, all anxiety is mostly the same. Sure, the subject matter might be different, but the process of creating anxiety is mostly consistent. And it's this process that is most important. Why? Because understanding the process, rather than giving your anxiety's content too much attention, helps you understand the need for exposure and reality-based beliefs. This is your ticket to outsmarting it and making your anxiety getaway!

* **False Belief:** I need my significant other to understand what I'm going through.

* **Reality-Based Belief:** Why? Although the understanding might be nice, what can it really do for you? Maybe it could provide some support and encouragement, but that can be done by your significant other without really understanding it. Even if understanding is received, why do you *need* it to overcome your anxiety? Again, it might be nice, but you surely don't need it. Receiving the understanding of a significant other has never been shown as a factor in extinguishing one's

anxiety. Plus, as I mentioned in earlier chapters, this is *your* anxiety to own, and therefore yours to do something about. So do something about it! It's up to you, whether anybody understands it or not. Whether anybody supports or encourages you or not. Remember, you've got my support and encouragement throughout this book to keep you company and provide understanding on your fear-facing journey.

* **False Belief:** Anxiety defines who I am.

* **Reality-Based Belief:** Anxiety in no way defines who you are, any more than high cholesterol defines Darrel (a random high cholesterol-sufferer). No one is defined by anxiety. That's not to say that people's identities aren't wrapped up in their struggles. That's certainly true for many with anxiety. But that's a choice. You choose to make anxiety your identity. That doesn't mean it's who you are in reality. It is simply a syndrome, issue, or difficulty. Whatever you want to call it, you're much more than anxiety.

Anxiety Getaway Tip

False beliefs are not based on facts (I hope that's obvious by now!). They are based on assumptions, mistruths, habitual perspectives, and sometimes outright lies that require correction to reduce anxiety. Modifying false beliefs for reality-based beliefs changes the way you behave, respond to, and experience life itself. No soon-to-be-shattered fantasies. No illusions. No destructive belief systems. To get on the path toward claiming your calm, start focusing on plain old, honest-to-goodness truth!

STEPS TO REALITY

It's now time to discuss the exact steps necessary to identify and exchange your false beliefs for reality-based beliefs—to ensure your anxiety getaway! For clarification along the way, I've referenced Nara's journey toward overcoming her fear of making mistakes. While reading, keep your own anxiety and probable false beliefs in mind! Here we go:

1. **Purchase a log book** of some kind to label your *False Belief Journal*. You can use an app or the notes function of your smartphone, if you prefer. The idea is to maintain a log for identifying and examining your false beliefs, as well as your reality-based responses. It will operate as both a worksheet/diary and a record to turn to for a dose of reality, when mired in a false belief you've already addressed and countered.

2. **Start with any area of anxiety you'd like**, though it's best to just start with what plagues you the most. Identify your anxiety. What makes you anxious? Again, as with exposure, you must determine what scares you. Write this down. Nara feared making mistakes.

3. **Use reverse engineering**. I do not mean getting on a train and walking backward. I mean identifying when you're anxious and *working* backward to determine your underlying false beliefs. Your anxiety is the indicator that false beliefs are in action. Explore what you believe about your anxiety-provoking experience. Nara began paying

attention to her anxious suffering over the prospect of making mistakes. She soon realized that she believed mistakes would only result in "bad things happening."

4. **Pepper yourself with questions**. This is key in changing your false beliefs. Become a skeptic around the subject of your fear. Questions are one of the most powerful strategies in the fight against false beliefs, as they chip away at their illusion and strength. False beliefs can be so strong that it's like being under a spell. When under it, conscious awareness is a challenge. You don't know what you don't know. You don't know you're acting in accordance with false belief. However, the right questions can break that spell. To claim your calm, your anxiety-promoting false beliefs have to change! So begin a regular routine of asking the following specific questions to identify and challenge your false beliefs. Then work to exchange them for reality-based beliefs!

Questions Designed to Break The Spell of Anxiety-Producing False Beliefs:

1. **Is what I believe true?** From a factual standpoint, is what you fear reality-based? In Nara's case, was it true that making a mistake always resulted in "bad things happening"?

2. **What am I thinking?** As we've already established, there is no anxiety without belief. It is your false beliefs that move you into fear. In other words, if you didn't

believe that what you fear could cause you harm, anxiety would not exist. Complicating matters further, beliefs are often buried under an avalanche of anxious thoughts (to be discussed more in the OCD chapter). While underlying beliefs create and perpetuate anxiety, it is unreasonable thoughts that can provide them distracting cover, leaving you unaware. Thoughts that throw people are often of the "What If" variety, such as, "What if I panic?", "What if I lose control?", "What if they laugh at me?", "What if I'm trapped!", and the like. Some of these sound like beliefs, but beliefs are the underlying core perspective driving these anxious thought-based stories in your head. One strategy to uncover your false beliefs is to first identify what you're thinking. For instance, Nara's thoughts were fixated on the potentially destructive results she imagined would follow possible mistakes. Thoughts like, "What if I fail?" and "What if I destroy my entire life?" plagued her.

3. **Where is the proof?** Look at the data. Get scientific. Become like a researcher. What does the data point to? Is there proof that this belief is true? What data substantiates what you believe is true? For Nara, where was the proof that making a mistake always led to "bad things happening"? What data substantiated this? There wasn't any. Trusting your anxious feelings without seeking real world data is often the very foundation of false beliefs.

4. **Are there deeper false beliefs associated
with my main false belief?** Some of our
false beliefs are so entrenched, they can be
a challenge to root out. Nara's primary false
belief was that mistakes always result in
"bad things happening." But were there any
deeper beliefs creating further anxiety?

To go beyond your basic anxiety-provoking
false beliefs to identify and dismantle more
entrenched false beliefs, you must *break them
down with associations*. To do so, take a look at
what you associate with your fear. Does it have to
do with certain desires? Does it have to do with
life lessons you picked up along the way? Does
it have to do with how you see yourself? Does it
have to do with how others see you? Ask these
deeper questions. They'll bear fruit the deeper
you go. Examine what you believe about the fear
itself. Examine what you believe about yourself
related to this fear. Examine what you believe
about the world and other people. Examine it all!
For instance, with a deeper look, we discovered
that Nara associated her critical mother with
her fear of mistakes. This led to the discovery
that she believed if she made a mistake, she was
less than, and even worse, that people would be
disappointed in her and reject her as incapable.
This, she believed, she could not accept or handle.
All false, by the way!

* **Am I anxious about the present?** One indicator
false beliefs are promoting your anxiety is that
it's rarely present-based. Think about it. Anxiety
is usually future-based, as in "what if" this
happens, "what if" that happens. Anxiety can
also be past-based, hoping that what happened

before does not happen again. Anxiety often feels like a four-alarm fire. Like a real-time, drop-everything-because-you've-got-to-fend-for-your-life emergency. Like something terrible is about to happen. Any. Damn. Minute. But anxiety is rarely, if ever, a true and present danger. Why? Because, again, anxiety tends to be a past- or future-focused experience. Both are illusions. The past is nothing but a memory. And the future? It hasn't even occurred.

Consider a real emergency. Though the experience is intense and adrenalized, there isn't really any anxiety during the actual emergency. Why? Because we tend to be present when handling a real emergency. Fully in the moment. With our survival instinct triggered, we experience the surge of adrenaline and do our best to deal with what is confronting us.

For example, if you're driving and a car crosses the center divider heading straight for you, you wouldn't think, "Boy, am I anxious. This car is about to ram me head on. I don't know what's going to happen. This sure is frightening." Instead, you'd be completely present. Your survival instinct would kick in and you would handle that current and very real emergency by swerving with all you've got. Many of my patients reveal having always been curious why, when in a real emergency, they tend to respond well. However, when nothing is truly dangerous, they can feel like they're anxiously falling apart. This is why!

More proof of anxiety's illusion is its typical arrival *after* the emergency is over and the person is now safe. Once the real emergency has passed, an anxious story can be formed and fed. Pertaining to the above example, a story might be, "Oh my gosh, I almost died! Maybe driving isn't so necessary? Come to think of it, I have had my eye on the pleasures of being a bus rider." Anxiety is the story in your head, and anxious stories are not real, living, present-moment experiences. If you look carefully, they consist of false beliefs. Therefore, once again, anxiety is an illusion.

* **Am I accepting what is?** Another way of considering that which is reality-based is by accepting what truly is. Not what you think it is, or how you think it should be. Not your opinion. But what, in reality, *just is*. For example, weather is neither good nor bad. It just is. That doesn't mean it can't be destructive and that you would prefer it in a different form. And yet, there are countless people that place a value judgment on it or falsely believe it shouldn't be the case. For example, "It's not supposed to rain on my birthday!" is a common complaint. I think you'll agree that "supposed to" has nothing to do with it!

Part of our vernacular is to say, "It is what it is." Unfortunately, this phrase is often improperly used to describe a situation that a person is defeated by and doesn't like, not one they're accepting for its reality. The truth of the phrase speaks to accepting *what is* because we cannot do anything about it. Ironically, accepting *what is* then frees us to focus on what we can do. For example, Nara feared making mistakes on papers, tests, and in life. Prior to treatment, she practiced the false belief that she could avoid all mistakes, which only led to ever-increasing anxiety. This did not change until she chose to accept *what is*. The fact was that no matter how hard she tried to avoid them, errors would occur from time to time. Her acceptance of this reality finally allowed her to focus on learning.

5. Practice **identifying other people's false beliefs** as training and inspiration for identifying yours. Consider the conflicts of people familiar to you. What problems do they have? What false beliefs might they hold about life, people, or themselves? For example, when Nara began using this strategy, she first considered her friend Marcus, who often criticized her and others. Hiding behind "just being honest," his rude remarks often hurt those closest to him. Nara realized Marcus had a false belief that sharing his unfiltered thoughts was justified and fair in close relationships. Needless to say, Marcus pushed lots of people away. As stated, beliefs have consequences! That said, being able to identify her friend's false belief and observe its impact on his life was great practice for identifying her own.

6. Practice **consistently**. Make exchanging your false beliefs for reality-based beliefs a consistent practice or you'll experience the anxious consequences. You can't just chip away at some false beliefs for a couple weeks, stop, and expect others not to crop up or old ones not to rear their ugly heads. You've got to continue to practice, otherwise you'll forget. It's a little like learning a language. Use it or lose it. This reminds me of an anecdote I heard about Buddhists in conflict with each other for sniffling during meditation periods. Even at a mountain monastery in a structured,

quiet life of meditation, it's necessary to consistently practice acceptance of *what is* and maintain a reality-based belief system. After all, everyone knows that reality states: even people who stop and smell the roses sometimes get runny noses.

7. **Don't mistake positive thinking for reality-based beliefs**. While fighting her anxiety, Nara tried practicing positive thinking by telling herself, "I don't make mistakes. I always do great." This led to a groundswell of greater negativity when she did make an error. All based on false belief.

   Most people love the idea of positive thinking. And while it has its merits, they give it way too much value. Though I support positive thinking to a point, it's always best to side with reality! The problem with positive thinking is that there is no positive without the negative. The more you make a concerted effort to think positive, the more negative your thinking will be. Remember, whatever you resist, persists. Go ahead and practice positive thinking, but when you catch yourself struggling to do so, that's an indication that you're wrestling with a false belief. Right then and there, transition to reality-based thinking.

8. **Remember, anxiety is an indicator of false beliefs**. When anxious, address your beliefs without hesitation. Seek them out. You'll find they're there! Correct them by following the steps I've included. Keep challenging your false beliefs with reality and you'll soon believe reality. Believing reality? What a concept!

BIDDING FAREWELL TO YOUR FALSE BELIEFS

In addition to exposure, cultivating a regular practice of reality-based belief is the most powerful anxiety treatment strategy available. Consider it an anxiety corrective. First, when it comes to anxiety, the hammer of reality can challenge your false fear messages and stop them from taking you down the rabbit hole of anxious suffering. Second, moving forward, a reality-based belief practice can prevent false fear messages from even percolating, so you stop them before they start. And third, as a life management skill, the more you customarily engage in reality-based beliefs, the less anxious you'll find yourself day to day. You'll handle former anxiety-provoking situations from the calmest, most empowered position possible—accepting what is, while taking solution-focused actions when possible.

In the following chapters, we'll be combining exposure and the transition to reality-based beliefs for a knockout punch to some of the most common anxiety issues. Whether you struggle with panic, a phobia, or OCD, you'll receive further lessons on specific exposure exercises and reality-based beliefs boiled down to their essence. These are all designed to help you make your anxiety getaway. Let's keep moving, so you can claim your calm!

CHAPTER 7

THE PANIC ATTACK COMEBACK

"Growth demands a temporary surrender of security."

—**Gail Sheehy**

"Don't freak out!"

—**Unknown author**

Right out of the gate, I must address the most important lesson of this chapter. And that is... There's no such thing as a panic attack! There, I said it. Yes, I know society will tell you differently and that you've been conditioned to believe this notion, too. But what you call "panic" is simply an adrenaline surge. That's it! What you're experiencing is adrenaline! Nothing more. There's no such thing as a panic attack. However, because I understand you probably call this struggle a "panic attack," I'll use the terms "panic," "panic attack," and "panic disorder" throughout this chapter for the sake of clarity and ease.

LET'S UNPACK A PANIC ATTACK

Your first panic attack probably arrived without warning, as most panic attacks do. More than likely, this experience was initiated by an intense amount of stress building in your life. First-time panic attacks are often preceded by the sense of being overwhelmed. Here is the typical sequence from which many initial panic attacks are derived:

Unaware of steadily increasing stress and lacking healthy coping methods, the survival instinct is falsely triggered (in no real emergency) with a strong unexpected adrenaline surge (courtesy of the fight-or-flight protective process). For many when this happens, unless they have the skills to handle their stress and interpret it properly, a panic attack erupts. And it can happen anytime, anywhere. When it does occur, the mind searches for control due to a lack of understanding and awareness over this adrenaline dump. Without any real external danger present to explain the internal upheaval, the "panicker" assigns a danger label to this unfamiliar adrenalized surge.

It's the false danger label we assign these situations that encourages anxiety. Trouble arises when you label an adrenaline surge as "wrong" or as an experience that should not be occurring. Bodies have sensations, many of which you can't control. Of course, it's natural to wonder why you've been slammed by this uncomfortable physical experience *seemingly* out of the blue. However, inaccurately labeling this adrenalized moment as "panic" and adding a terrifying fictional narrative is your invitation for more.

If not handled quickly with awareness and specific strategies, more panic attacks can follow. Unfortunately, your desire to get rid of the adrenaline response, and the tendency to fight it because it makes you uncomfortable, only digs you deeper into the experience of panic. Panic attacks are described as a period of intense fear with several symptoms that can vary from person to person.

Symptoms of a "Panic Attack"

(Most people have at least four.)[1]

* Pounding heart, quickened or rapid heart rate, or heart palpitations. Many feel like their heart is bursting out of their chest or fear they're about to have a heart attack. This can also include chest pain and tightness.

* Sudden sweating and perspiring. Some feel suddenly warm or experience a hot flash.

* Feeling like you're trembling and shaking all over. Some describe this as feeling extremely jittery.

* Feeling short of breath. Many feel like they can't breathe or fear they're going to stop breathing.

* Feeling like you're choking.

* Feeling nauseated, or experiencing stomach pain and discomfort.

* Dizziness. Some feel very light-headed, like they're going to pass out.

* Feeling cold. Having the chills.

* Numbness or tingling in the hands or feet (paresthesia).

* Derealization. This is feeling like you're detached from, or outside of, reality.

* Depersonalization. This is feeling like you're detached from, or outside of, yourself.

* Feeling like you're going insane.

* Feeling like you're losing control of yourself.
* Feeling like you're about to die.

Although panic attacks can be very frightening for all who suffer from them, they're highly treatable. In fact, they're not as difficult to overcome as you might think! Because the proper treatment for panic attacks focuses on one particularly powerful strategy, treatment doesn't have to be lengthy either. As long as you do the homework, suffering from panic attacks can soon be a distant memory (though not one you'd be glad to keep snapshots of in a photo album).

I always find it unfortunate when a patient suffering from panic attacks has wasted time and money on trips to the emergency room, medication, or on regular talk therapy. None of these can resolve panic attacks. That said, it's understandable many to go to the hospital or a medical doctor initially. Most fear they're having a medical problem or life-threatening issue, given that panic attack symptoms mimic heart trouble and the like. But because medical doctors are not anxiety treatment experts, they have little to offer those struggling other than benzodiazepines (e.g., Xanax, Ativan, Klonopin, Valium) that sedate you for the time being. To make matters worse, these meds are addictive. To top it off, they also reinforce the avoidance pattern. The more you ingest them, the more you teach your brain that the only way to handle these sensations is to escape with a tranquilizing pill, along with engaging in your other evasive methods.

To be fair, until you learn how to handle the adrenaline, it can be challenging to tolerate without the release that accompanies fighting off an external attacker or running for your life in a real emergency. Still, although you've been biologically set up to avoid discomfort, it's your "horrifying, I must stop this now" labeling of the uncomfortable experience that provides the rocket fuel for your bumpy panic ride.

Your symptoms are all adrenaline-based, with the exception of feelings such as "It feels like I'm going to die" (those are based on your labels). The sensations are designed to protect us by preparing our bodies to fight for our lives or run like hell. For example, chills and tingling sensations are a result of blood rushing from your extremities to your trunk for strength and balance. Unfortunately, when one experiences these powerful sensations, a misinterpretation can lead to panic as a reaction.

Ultimately, it is one's thoughts that create a panic attack, as one can incorrectly respond to the sensations of adrenaline by labeling them alarmingly dangerous. This belief of "danger" then creates more anxious thoughts and symptoms, leading to a panic attack.

The usual pattern of response is to fear having another attack. You may even begin to avoid places and situations where the attack occurred. Makes sense, right? After all, you don't like to feel out of control (most of us humans hate that!). Unfortunately, avoidance only serves to encourage more panic attacks. Plus, the more you experience them, the more they can spread to other areas of your life and world like a raging brushfire. This is also why agoraphobia often accompanies ongoing panic attacks. Panic attacks can shut down your life...if you let them.

PANIC DISORDERED?

Though I'm not a supporter of the diagnostic label, in my field, ongoing panic attacks are called *panic disorder*. Panic disorder is defined by at least a month of frequent, abrupt panic attacks with a fear of having others, a tendency to avoid situations or experiences where panic attacks have occurred (leading to a lack of freedom), and an extreme concern about what the panic attacks might imply or manifest (e.g., loss of control, sanity, death).

The easiest way to understand the cause of continuing panic attacks is to say that panic disorder is born of a fear of fear. More often than not, due to the intense, unexpected adrenaline experience one undergoes during their first panic attack, one then believes that something is wrong, falsely labels it "bad," and then fears having another. This false belief erroneously teaches your brain that it needs to protect you from this adrenaline-based experience via false fear messages. These then trigger the survival instinct's fight-or-flight mechanism. Ironically, this means your brain is now protecting you from adrenaline in the manner which you've unintentionally taught it—by sending more adrenaline! Big oops!

This fear of having another panic attack is really just a fear of experiencing the adrenalized bodily sensations that you associate with danger—rapid heartbeat, sudden warmth or sweating, dizziness, shallow breathing, tingling in the hands and feet, and more. Unfortunately, the more you *fear* panic, the greater the likelihood that you'll panic, as you've now taught your brain to fear this adrenaline surge. And you've attached a fear-inducing story to the experience to boot! Once again, this means that your brain is sending false fear messages that indicate you're in jeopardy—from your own body and mind! It's a bit like the psychological equivalent of an autoimmune disorder, where the body attacks itself in an effort to help itself, due to a systemic glitch. And once you fear fear, you'll start seeking these symptoms to ascertain whether they're present, thereby creating them in the process! As you've now learned, fighting will only increase adrenaline!

Panic disorder develops with disconcertingly speedy style. Primarily, because panic attacks are so frightening for most people, they never want to have one again, and do all they can to dodge their so-called foreboding sensations. Unfortunately, without the proper help and treatment, worrying about having panic attacks unwittingly encourages more of them. This then creates panic disorder, also known as a fear of fear. Again, the main struggle with panic disorder is not only repeated, spontaneous panic attacks, but a tendency to worry about having more. This ensures many days filled with adrenaline surges, and in between, straight up anxiety.

When Brian, an athlete in his forties, arrived in my office, he had been suffering from daily panic attacks for five months. Not surprisingly, the experience had dramatically interfered with his life. He had taken a leave of absence from his long-held job at an accounting firm. His marriage was in shambles (partly because, up to this point, he had refused to seek proper help). His reliance on Ativan furthered his marital conflict, as he was often sedated to try avoiding all that could trigger stress or fear. In addition to his panic attacks, this mental state made him even more unavailable to his children. His friendships were also severely compromised, as he declined all invitations for fear of having a panic attack and being embarrassed. He had also completely curtailed training for triathlons with his wife. He refused to participate. All aspects of exercise now frightened him due to the resulting increased heart rate and feelings of "dizziness." Though it was his favorite activity in the past, swimming now terrified him the most. He felt this probably had to do with his first panic attack that struck him while swimming in the ocean.

Brian's fears consumed every aspect of his life. He was terrified of being dizzy and having a heart attack, no matter the location. Though he felt a bit safer at home, every morning upon awakening, he checked to determine if he felt any signs of dizziness or chest pain. And he most assuredly did, each and every time! In fact, his self-evaluations infiltrated other aspects of his day, to the point that he was in a constant battle.

Brian had come to equate these sensations with impending death. The feared tightness in his chest led him to the emergency room on more than a few occasions. Brian needed help fast! To his credit, he was aware his life was being consumed by fear. Finally, his concern over his crumbling relationship with his family motivated him to commit to exposure and false belief modification.

It's easy to imagine how frequent panic attacks can interfere with and even shut down one's life. For example, as described with Brian, most people with panic disorder fear entering situations in which they've previously panicked. They also fear situations where they feel trapped with no easy escape, or where help is not accessible. This, by the way, is the very theme of agoraphobia (to be discussed soon).

As with all existing anxiety syndromes, avoidance is the common destructive strategy used to cope with persistent panic attacks. This, of course, shuts down quality of life even further.

The good news is that none of the above need continue if you practice the anxiety getaway methods in this chapter. With a little elbow grease, you can become adept at handling adrenaline surges and claim your calm.

THE PANIC ATTACK SMACK ATTACK

It's time to focus on the exact steps necessary to stop any panic attack in its tracks, so you can make your anxiety getaway. As always, this scientifically proven anxiety treatment is twofold, with its focus on changing false beliefs and simultaneous engagement in exposure. Exposure to panic involves facing feared adrenaline sensations through homework assignments designed to encourage your brain to adapt or "get used to" this bodily response. Then, rather than react with fear and a desire to escape, you can soon claim your calm!

As a refresher, exposure desensitizes your brain to fear (which began with a false belief) by extinguishing its false fear messages. However, if you haven't changed your anxiety-establishing false beliefs to reality-based beliefs, they will soon undo your exposure work. With dangerously looming sustained false beliefs, you'll encourage avoidance again and, like a house of cards, eventually your brain will respond to protect you with the return of false fear messages! Back to where you began.

Exposure and false belief modification must go hand in hand. Just as exposure is not enough without changing false beliefs, it is the same in reverse. When false fear messages are in effect, changing false beliefs isn't enough without exposure, either. The brain's false fear messages can be so strong, they'll override attempts to respond rationally with reality-based belief in the moment. So again, effective anxiety treatment is twofold: exposure work *and* modification of false beliefs! Moving on...

To overcome panic attacks you must expose yourself to what you fear. And because you fear what you call "panic," this means you must expose yourself to triggers from within. This is a little different than exposure to a phobia, which is often focused on external fears. Panic is defined by anxiety over the internal. In other words, fear of bodily sensations and thoughts like, "I'm going to die," "I'm losing control," and so on.

Are you ready to rid your life of panic attacks and make your anxiety getaway? Let's begin with your one and only exposure assignment to banish panic.

Here is your key exposure assignment to claim your calm. For 90 percent of the panic sufferers I've treated, those that followed this assignment for two weeks straight either achieved their anxiety getaway or were very close to doing so! Remember, seventeen hours is the average amount of time required for the brain to adapt to a particular fear. And with panic there is only one level. So, with this exercise it will likely be less, if done correctly. It was for Brian (as it has been for countless others). It took Brian twelve days to resolve his panic attacks, and he was as terrified as anybody I've treated. His willingness to start his exposure and see it through paid off. If you're struggling with panic, it's time to start yours. So let's get to it!

Follow the Exact Steps of this Exposure to Claim Your Calm from Panic Attacks

1. First, choose the panic symptom you fear most. Or choose the top two you feel launch

you into full freak-out mode. It could be, like Brian, that you fear dizziness and potentially passing out, in addition to having a heart attack. Just pick the top one or two as your exposure focus.

2. Remember imaginal exposure? As a reminder, this is exposure using your imagination (for a full refresher, return to chapter 5 as needed). You are now going to act out your top symptom, as if it's happening right now. You don't have to be Al Pacino or Meryl Streep to do so—just do your best to imagine your symptom occurring with the utmost intensity. Play pretend as you might have as a child. Using your imagination, play it dramatically, like an actor's death scene. You're going to induce your symptom and encourage it to the extreme. I want you to increase it. Don't allow it to just take up space. In other words, incite it. Take your symptom to its worst extent. For example, if you fear dizziness, I want you to imagine you're as dizzy as possible. You couldn't be any dizzier! The room is spinning! Try to make yourself pass out. Think you're passing out. Literally try to make it happen. Tell yourself your vision is nothing but a blur. Imagine the experience is happening now. Feel it! You're walking like a drunk in a tornado. Tell yourself, "I'm going to pass out. I'm so dizzy. Everything is spinning and a-whirling. Oh no, I'm going to pass out!"

Do the same with any panic symptom you fear. If you fear a heart attack, imagine your heart seizing right now.

Better still, think of it bursting out of your chest. Foster a sense of pain in your heart. Feel it tightening with teeth-grinding agony. Get the picture?

3. Now, with whatever symptom you've identified as the foundation of your panic fears, I want you to purposely incite and increase it six times a day. You read that right! I want you to have six panic attacks a day! Force your most feared panic symptom on purpose! Sure, it will be a little scary. But soon you'll find that what occurs is the opposite of what you expect. Without your typical resistance to panic symptoms, there is nowhere for your anxiety to land. Without the fight, there is no panic. You'll see! Then, it's only a matter of time before your adrenaline surges dissipate when not required for a real emergency. But only if you follow the instructions to the letter and actually do the exposure! Do the work and reap the reward.

4. Keep each panic exposure alive for as long as you can in that moment, until you can't force the symptom any longer. Your goal should be a time length of <u>at least three minutes</u>, but try for more. Escalate your symptom to epically terrible proportions. Increase and amplify it until your head is popping off (figuratively, of course—I've never been one to support headlessness as a cure for anxiety). For example, if you're afraid of trembling, purposely shake all over. Imagine it's uncontrollable. Try to make yourself feel as shaky as possible. Encourage the thought that you can't stop trembling. If you struggle

with your hands shaking when panicked, hold a cup and pretend you're unable to take a sip. Shake until you can't push it any further in that moment. Stop when you feel you've taken it to its fullest extent with that particular exposure, but not before performing it for at least three minutes. Do this six times a day with your most feared symptom, for the next two weeks.

5. Keep a tally of each panic exposure. You're done for the day when you arrive at six. Do not ignore this tallying step. It's important for a couple of reasons. First, it adds structure to your exposure. It provides you with a sense of completion and accomplishment over panic per day. This will help you earn steadily increasing confidence when facing your adrenaline. But second, and more importantly, this step teaches your brain that you are deliberately forcing panic. Remember, you've erroneously taught your brain to protect you from the adrenaline experience by labeling it as dangerous, then fighting it. And how is your brain playing bodyguard? By sending false fear messages that trigger...more adrenaline. So essentially, you're unwittingly lighting a fire, hoping to use it to fight that very fire. Adding insult to injury, you've attached a story to your panic experience full of false beliefs that sustain it (We'll get to these shortly). However, with this exposure, you're now challenging your false fear messages in order to extinguish them. You're turning the tables on panic by welcoming your symptoms, all in order to help your brain adapt to your fear-inducing

thoughts about adrenaline. To overcome panic attacks, you need your brain to become indifferent. And the path to this achievement is exposure. Tally-ho!

6. Get your six panic attacks completed early in the day, if you're able. Consider it like exercising. Sometimes, if you don't get your workout done early, it's easy to slough off a trip to the gym at night. But despite your schedule, be disciplined! Follow through with your six panic attacks a day, no matter what.

7. To be crystal clear, do not wait around for a panic attack to strike before you do your exposure. You've got six panic attacks a day to complete, so get to them. Seek out your panic symptoms. Induce them. Conjure and create them, especially when you're totally calm. This is exposure time! You've got to go after it.

8. In case you're wondering, you must also do this assignment when you actually *feel* panic! Fighting any panic attack will only undo the exposure progress you've made with your imaginal work. How could it help if you resist when you're actually panicking? Remember, that's what created false fear messages and got you into this mess in the first place! Never fight these symptoms. Instead, when panicked, follow these same exposure steps. Say, "Bring it on!" Then tally it up!

9. When engaged in this exposure, you might find it a challenge to encourage panic when you're in a calmer state. This is nothing to

worry about. Just do your best to conjure up that panic anxiety. Use your imagination and escalate your feared symptoms. It doesn't matter if you're unable to match even close to the degree of your exact experience when panicking. All that matters is you are exposing yourself to your sensations deliberately, until your brain is desensitized to them and your false fear messages are extinguished. So just get this exposure done! Two weeks, six forced panic attacks a day— on purpose! That's it!

FROM PANIC TO FALSE BELIEF MECHANIC

In addition to your panic exposure, as you've now learned, you must also focus on adopting reality-based beliefs. Ultimately, it is your false beliefs that are responsible for your descent into a panic attack. And these false beliefs also perpetuate your fear of more attacks.

Below, I cover the common false beliefs that most panic sufferers hold, followed by the reality-based correctives to practice. Take a look to see if they match yours. If you're able, be sure to identify other false panic beliefs you maintain, along with the reality to counter them. Enough said. It's time to take a ride on Truth Boulevard. So get that mental wrench ready and review the following for your false belief overhaul.

To Fully Overcome Panic Attacks, Modify These False Beliefs

* **False Belief:** I'm having a panic attack.

* **Reality-Based Belief:** Again, there is no such thing! It's an adrenaline surge you're incorrectly associating with danger. You are mislabeling adrenaline. And unfortunately, if you're fearful of frequent unexpected adrenaline surges, you've most likely become hypervigilant, searching for signs of "panic" with the desire to control them (like Brian). This search always backfires because it's in response to believing the false fear messages instructing you of danger. These then trigger the survival instinct's fight-or-flight adrenaline response again and again. As a reminder, you've unintentionally taught your brain to protect you from your own adrenaline by trying to avoid it, setting this cycle in motion. The more you fight it, the more you increase your adrenaline response, transitioning you into an even greater wave, which you call a panic attack.

* **False Belief:** When I panic, it means something is "bad" or "wrong."

* **Reality-Based Belief:** Your panic is occurring because you're labeling the adrenaline response as "bad" or "wrong"! You may recall from earlier chapters that if you misinterpret adrenaline based on excitement, uncertainty, or energy, you will label it a problem. This false belief teaches your brain that adrenaline itself is a threat. Your brain will then protect you from this adrenaline experience via this false fear message—with an increase in adrenaline! You'll then interpret your adrenaline surge as an even larger problem and fight it more, attaching stories of terror in the process. Talk about a messed up cycle of false beliefs and false fear messages! And it all began with some faulty labeling.

Why assign a label of doom to a sensation that is part of your system's wiring? Those with ADHD don't define their hyperactivity as doom, and that's another form of energy. So don't assign a negative label to your adrenaline. It is what it is.

* **False Belief:** Exercise makes me panic. I should stop for now.

* **Reality-Based Belief:** Sometimes people who fear panic are afraid of exercise, as it can mimic the adrenaline response (again, like Brian). Symptoms such as sweating, rapid heartbeat, labored breathing, and more, remind them of their panic experience. But exercise for those who fear panic can be fantastic exposure! So if you fear exercise, dive in! Wading in is fine, too. If you prefer, start slow with just a few minutes of walking. Increase distance once you consistently reach a level of one or zero on the anxiety scale, as your brain adapts (see chapter 5 for more, if a refresher is needed!). Avoiding exercise will reinforce fear of your adrenaline symptoms.

If you typically exercise in a gym, part of your resistance can also be based on a desire to avoid public embarrassment should you have a panic attack. For those with panic disorder with agoraphobia, a gym can have added pressure due to its social nature with regard to status, competition, dating, and friendship opportunities. Heading to the gym can be an exposure exercise in its own right.

* **False Belief:** I have a disorder.

* **Reality-Based Belief:** "Panic disorder" is a diagnostic label for those with ongoing panic attacks. But it's not really a disorder. This term implies that it's a malady you can't resolve, and

certainly not quickly. This is simply untrue! If you follow the two week exposure I described earlier in this chapter, you'll be well on your way to your anxiety getaway! Of course, if you don't, you won't. It's up to you.

* **False Belief:** When having a panic attack, I feel like I might die or have a psychotic break.

* **Reality-Based Belief:** The experience of panic itself cannot kill you or cause you to lose your mind (even though I know it feels like it can). In fact, by reading this now, you have proved this. Panic attacks are just uncomfortable. Remember, they're just an adrenaline surge. And by the way, there is no such thing as a "nervous breakdown" (even though The Rolling Stones have a great song about someone who's had nineteen of them!). The term was often used in the '60s due to a lack of familiarity with anxiety and depressive symptoms. So those struck by a "nervous breakdown" were really suffering from panic attacks, OCD, depression, or some combination thereof.

* **False Belief:** I think a quick-fix method will work for me.

* **Reality-Based Belief:** No other methods have been scientifically proven to work for panic attacks, phobias, or OCD other than the CBT methods noted in this book. Unproven and ineffective methods like breathing exercises, special diets, hypnosis, EMDR, or other "quick fixes" sold online, cannot cure panic attacks, despite what some might suggest. Traditional talk therapy has also been shown to be ineffective in treating anxiety. Nothing but facing fear and

modifying false beliefs that perpetuate anxiety can cure anxiety. It's only logical!

* **False Belief:** I need anti-anxiety medication to overcome my "panic attacks."

* **Reality-Based Belief:** Your panic struggle can be resolved naturally without dangerous addictive medications that add fuel to the fire! There is no pill that can treat fear.

Due to physicians lack of knowledge regarding how to treat panic attacks, they often prescribe benzodiazepines such as Ativan, Xanax, Klonopin, and Valium (also known as tranquilizers or sedatives). These are extremely addictive and have intense, potentially dangerous withdrawal symptoms. Unbeknownst to the medical doctor and patient, they also serve to keep the cycle of panic attacks going by teaching the brain (again) that the only way to handle the experience is to escape. This serves to bolster false fear messages! Not exactly beneficial.

Not only do these "anti-anxiety" meds encourage more anxiety over time, they also create an addiction. One caveat is the prescription of certain antidepressants prescribed for anxiety by psychiatrists. Antidepressants appear to reduce a degree of anxiety, but again, cannot totally resolve it. They seem most appropriate for those struggling with such a high degree of anxiety that it's interfering with their functioning and ability to complete exposure assignments.

* **False Belief:** The goal for my self-help anxiety treatment is to never panic again.

* **Reality-Based Belief:** That desire is understandable, but it belies fear. Being uncomfortable (also known as afraid) with having a panic attack is going to encourage more panic

attacks. The goal is to be unafraid of an adrenaline surge, and ultimately, confident in your ability to manage the experience anywhere, at any time. Remember, anxiety is created and encouraged by fighting it through your battle, your resistance. You must accept the sensations. Welcome them if they occur. Maybe even love the adrenaline because it's part of you? Okay, maybe that's a tall order for some. But you could appreciate the fact that adrenaline serves several functions. Whether it's based on excitement, energy, uncertainty, or fear, adrenaline can be an indicator that you're leading a stimulating life! The reality is, you're a human being with capabilities, feelings, sensations, and this amazing brain that can do such wonderful things—even if it sometimes makes mistakes by accepting the false lessons we teach it!

CHAPTER 8

HAVING A PHOBIA IS NO UTOPIA

"Nothing in life is to be feared, it is only to be understood. Now is the time to understand more, so that we may fear less."

—Marie Curie

"A lot of people are afraid of heights. Not me, I'm afraid of widths."

—Steven Wright

It's time to discuss phobias. Without labeling them, we've already addressed many throughout this book, including fear of public speaking (glossophobia), fear of flying (aviophobia), fear of dogs (cynophobia), fear of clowns (coulrophobia), fear of night (nyctophobia), fear of dating (sarmassophobia), and more. Below is a list of other phobias for your identification, edification, enlightenment, and maybe entertainment.

Additional Phobias[1]

(Though not all, due to the vastness of what we human beings can fear.)

Fear of heights (acrophobia), fear of small spaces (claustrophobia), fear of spiders (arachnophobia), fear of bridges (gephyrophobia), fear of traveling by car (hodophobia), fear of needles (aichmophobia), fear of blood (hemophobia), fear of cats (ailurophobia), fear of water (hydrophobia), fear of birds (ornithophobia), fear of doctors (iatrophobia), fear of being alone (autophobia), fear of choking (anginophobia), fear of vomiting (emetophobia), fear of numbers (numerophobia), fear of sharks (selachophobia), fear of dolls (pediophobia), fear of knees (genuphobia), fear of mirrors (catoptrophobia), fear of belly buttons (omphalophobia).

Most of the fears mentioned so far have been what are called *specific phobias*. But there is a separate class of fears called *complex phobias*. These are somewhat more...complex. But their complex nature does not necessarily require a more complicated approach. In fact, you'll perform the same exposure strategies and steps detailed throughout chapter 5 , and the same false belief modification strategies from chapter 6, to treat them! The difference is simply that your exposure targets will be more extensive (we'll discuss details shortly).

In this chapter, I'm going to cover the two most common complex phobias: agoraphobia and social phobia. Just keep in mind, any time you need a full-fledged refresher on the strategies and steps of exposure, revisit chapter 5. It was designed, along with chapter 6 on modifying false beliefs, for you to return to again and again on your journey toward outsmarting your false fear messages and claiming your calm.

But back to the present! Let's now place a laser focus on phobias, first specific, then complex. All while keeping in mind the goal of you becoming heroic when phobic and making your anxiety getaway. Of course, first, we must define a phobia.

A PHOBIA BY ANY OTHER NAME

To put it simply (because why make it more complex, considering we'll soon discuss complex phobias!), a phobia is a fear of an object or situation that causes anxiety when encountered, anticipated, or even thought of, along with the creation of some degree of impairment or barrier in one's life. So, this really just describes a fear that interferes with life in some way.

For instance, Gemma and her cousin Lulu both feared spiders. However, Gemma had a phobia. Lulu did not. When both saw a spider, each screamed their lungs out. But that's where Lulu's arachnid terror ended and Gemma's only began.

Lulu's life was not inhibited by her fear of spiders. There was no impairment or barrier of any kind. Just some screaming when one was near. So she had a fear, but not a diagnosable phobia.

However, Gemma was consistently on the lookout for spiders, just for "safety." In fact, she often avoided certain rooms and most closets. When outside, she avoided tree-lined areas where there might be spiders and their accompanying webs. With spiders on her mind, if she anticipated heading into these areas or was pressured by circumstance to do so, she was intensely anxious. Now that's a phobia! In Gemma's life, these eight-legged insects took up tumultuous residence in her brain and impacted her choices.

But where did it begin?

COMMON ORIGINS OF A PHOBIA

No matter the beginning, remember: anxiety develops based on false belief, then avoidance, and then the production of false fear messages. Still, though they need water in the form of the process above to flourish, all phobias grow from one of the initial seedling experiences below:

1. A scary or threatening experience where one felt endangered. For example, a car accident can be a trigger.

2. An experience where one felt out of control or uncomfortable. Most who struggle with anxiety have an underlying difficulty in dealing with uncertainty or lack of control.

3. A fear intentionally or unintentionally taught by family members, usually during childhood. Growing up hearing about the false dangers of anything can have an impact.

4. A panic attack occurring during an activity (called a panic-induced phobia) can propel some to consider avoiding that activity.

STOP PHOBIA SHUTDOWN

As mentioned, we've discussed many phobias throughout this book, and they all have the potential to shut down life in one form or another. For example, Sally's bee phobia was interfering with her ability to be outdoors. Nara's fear of making mistakes was weaving its web throughout her life, creating a potential barrier to achievement.

Certain phobias can even have physically harmful effects. For example, people with a choking phobia can waste away due to avoiding food. People with needle phobia avoid having their blood drawn.

Thankfully, all phobias are treatable with exposure and the transition to reality-based beliefs! Whew!

On that note, here's a little exposure reminder if you're about to embark on your journey toward overcoming a phobia. The average amount of time required for your brain to adapt to each level of fear on your anxiety trigger list is seventeen hours. Keep these seventeen hours in mind as you make your way through your list. Put in as much consistent exposure time as you can until your brain becomes desensitized to those false fear messages and they're extinguished. Document your exposure time as you move through the process, and re-read chapter 5's strategies and steps as needed.

The quicker you engage in seventeen hours of exposure to your largest fear, the more quickly you can make your anxiety getaway (just remember you need to change your false beliefs, too!). And although seventeen hours might seem like a lot of fear-facing, like I've said, it's not even a full day!

That said, as mentioned in prior chapters, most prefer to manage their fear responses by engaging in gradual exposure to their largest anxiety triggers. That works equally well. Just move up your anxiety trigger list. Start with a fear that triggers a three on the anxiety scale. Or start even smaller. You set the pace.

Overcome Phobia with Motivation

To overcome a phobia, you've got to be motivated! How sick of anxiety are you? How is it disrupting your life? In what way has it interfered with your freedom? How does it limit you? What would you do if you didn't suffer from this particular phobia? You've got to be sick and tired of its barriers. Angry, even! Use that anger as energy and channel it into discipline to face discomfort with exposure. Outsmart those false fear messages and get on with it!

IT MEANS HOUSEBOUND, RIGHT?

There are many misconceptions about agoraphobia. For example, due to the Latin prefix, many believe it is a fear of open spaces. Though this can be a symptom, it's one I have rarely seen over the years, and it's certainly not the definition. Another misconception is that it is a fear of leaving your home. Though agoraphobia can result in this fear, especially in the most severe cases, this is also not the definition.

So what is it then?

Simply, agoraphobia is a fear of being trapped in a setting where one feels there is no quick escape or help immediately available.

As mentioned, because this fear can be triggered in a multitude of contexts, it is called a complex phobia. But it's not more complicated, just more involved and extensive. (Arguably, that does make it a bit more complicated to some.)

For many, when confronted by an agoraphobic fear, a panic attack can occur. Interestingly enough, a panic attack can also be the precursor to developing agoraphobia. This is due to a fear of having another panic attack and a tendency to avoid situations where they have occurred. Subsequently, one can begin to fear experiences where, in the event of panic, they can't escape quickly. For these reasons, panic attacks and agoraphobia can become inextricably linked. That said, even if panic attacks devolve into panic disorder, agoraphobia is not always an issue. Panic disorder and agoraphobia can be their own separate diagnoses, too.

Common Agoraphobic Fears and Symptoms

* Difficulty being out of one's comfort zone. Those with this phobia often have a certain radius in which they feel comfortable and do not move beyond it easily, if at all.

* Difficulty in crowds.

* Difficulty being away from home without their labeled support person, often a spouse or family member.

* Fear of places or enclosed spaces with no easy escape (along with fear of embarrassment should one panic). This typically results in one or more of the following: fear of flying, fear of traffic, fear of elevators, fear of being on a bus, and fear of driving over bridges. This also includes anxiety over weddings, waiting in a restaurant after ordering, riding a rollercoaster, and sitting in class or in a meeting.

* Fear of standing in line.

* Fear of travel.

* Fear of being in the rear of a large store or building with no exit in sight.

* Creation of excuses to avoid specific situations where you'll feel trapped, even as a passenger in a car.

* Fear of having panic attacks away from home.

* Anticipatory anxiety days or weeks before an event where you'll be expected to be away from your safety zone.

* Dependence on others driving you where needed, with a reduced ability to take care of your life on your own terms.

* Lack of freedom.

AGORAPHOBIA EXPOSURES FOR FEAR-FACING FUN

Here are my recommended exposure assignments. (Unless, of course, there is a pandemic. Then you'll have to wait.) While creating your anxiety trigger list from below, ignore those that don't generate anxiety. Be sure to include your own if not listed here. And remember to place these on a list from lowest to highest anxiety rating. Then, one by one, knock 'em down. Re-read chapter 5, if needed.

Here we go...

- ❐ Place yourself in enclosed spaces, such as movie theaters, grocery stores, shopping malls, and restaurants. For example, go to a restaurant by yourself and order a big meal. You might feel trapped waiting. When with company, sit on the inside seat in a booth or in any seating arrangement that sparks anxiety. Other similar exposure exercises include sitting in the middle of a crowded movie theater, or walking through an inside mall far from exits.
- ❐ Seek out crowds, such as at sporting events, concerts, and more.
- ❐ Travel away from home alone, to a place deemed far out of your comfort zone.
- ❐ In addition to driving, use public transportation, such as buses, trains, and planes.
- ❐ Attend social events, like parties, get-togethers, lunches, and more. These must be events you've avoided due to lack of an easy escape or fear of embarrassment, should a panic attack occur.
- ❐ Drive beyond a certain radius you have decided is safe.
- ❐ Stand in lines (at the bank, grocery store, etc.).
- ❐ Get stuck in traffic.
- ❐ Practice left-hand turns at traffic lights.
- ❐ Ride rollercoasters.
- ❐ Purposely spend time in the back of a department store, far away from exits.

- ❐ Stand in a crowded elevator. Go to a skyscraper and take a ride. Start off slowly, getting on and off at every other floor.

- ❐ Be alone without a support person.

A Few More Thoughts on Agoraphobia Exposure

When working on traveling out of your comfort zone, it's often useful to pick a destination as a goal you're working toward. Choose some locations you haven't driven to independently in a long while, perhaps related to activities you have missed or destinations you feel would enrich your life. Even if just errands, focus on those you'd like to do on your own, such as going to the bank, grocery store, or Target. Visit a relative or close friend you haven't seen much since your anxiety struggle began. Gradually work your way to these places. Again, start small. Maybe go 1/8 of the distance for a while, and then 1/4 of the distance for a while. Before you know it, you'll be there! Your brain will have adapted to that mileage. And remember, once you face some larger fears, some of the smaller fears can disappear.

- ✳ Remember seventeen hours. This is the average amount of time it takes for the brain to adapt to any level of fear. You might find some require just half that!

- ✳ If you're afraid of flying—not only due to distance away from home, but also because you fear feeling trapped on a plane—begin with a small flight. Maybe a forty-five minute flight to a small city. Yes, it can be expensive. Maybe do that twice a year. More, if you're able. Just start somewhere.

TRAPPED BY AGORAPHOBIC FALSE BELIEFS

Once your brain adapts to your anxiety-provoking stimuli (your scary, anxious situations), it will no longer trigger the fight-or-flight response that encourages your anxiety. But if you don't change the false beliefs that initially lit that fuse and subsequently supported your fear, you'll invite it all back!

Repeatedly practice correcting the following false beliefs, and explore any false beliefs you maintain that are not mentioned below. Be sure to add all of this to your journal for revisiting when caught in a false belief spiral.

* **False Belief:** When I'm far away from home, I can't take it. I have to escape to my comfort zone.

* **Reality-Based Belief:** There's nowhere to escape from or to. You can't run from yourself! That's exactly what you've been doing. You're running from internal sensations and false fear messages. You can become your own safety zone by making healthy choices informed by reality. The more you engage in exposure and the more you change your false beliefs, the more you'll realize you can tolerate far more than you ever knew. Once you claim your calm, you'll make decisions based on logic, not based on a need to escape what is inescapable—your own internal world.

* **False Belief:** But I *am* trapped in certain situations. Whether it's in traffic, on a plane, or stuck on a moving elevator. I can't just exit!

* **Reality-Based Belief:** While true you may not be able to leave when you please, the reality is you are misinterpreting danger. When anxious in

these situations, you are responding to false fear messages and not to what's in front of you. Being present in these scenarios wouldn't be anxiety-provoking otherwise.

* **False Belief:** There's no need to leave my comfort zone. I don't like to travel anyway.

* **Reality-Based Belief:** Living life isn't only about need. At least, it's not if you want to live a fulfilling one. But when mired in phobia, it becomes difficult to discern what one likes and doesn't like after a while. False fear messages and false beliefs toy with one's sense of reality and true nature. So in some way, you're a biased observer when it comes to your own life! At this point, you may not even know what you would enjoy if the barriers of anxiety were broken. You certainly owe it to yourself to face fear and find out!

Agoraphobia, though involved, is just like any fear. And fear can be conquered! You can outsmart agoraphobia. Being limited and confined to certain zones does not have to be your reality.

Now, let's get social!

WHAT IS SOCIAL PHOBIA?

Most people assume it's shyness or a preference for introversion—both aspects of personality. This is incorrect. Social phobia is an intense fear of social situations. The easiest and most definitive way to describe social phobia (also known as social anxiety) is a concern in the extreme for how others may evaluate you. In other words, it's a fear of being judged and caring too much about what other people think.

Social phobia is a complex phobia for a couple of reasons. First, unlike a specific phobia that manifests in only one area, social phobia manifests in many areas. For example, those who fear cats only struggle when they see cats or anticipate a cat encounter. However, social anxiety can arise at parties, at work, on the street, at grocery stores, in restaurants, with family, with strangers, and on and on. We are social beings living in a social world with lots of social opportunities. Second, social phobia is complex because it can incorporate other phobias. For example, those with social phobia can also fear sweating, blushing, or any other noticeable sign of anxiety they fear could be embarrassing or humiliating.

Research shows that social anxiety typically develops in adolescence and occurs over time. The feared social situations are either performance-based or interaction-based. Performance-based situations include experiences such as public speaking, class participation, or eating in front of others. An interaction-based situation can be attending a social event, meeting new people, dating, or talking on the phone. Like all anxiety syndromes, the feared social situation leads to avoidant behaviors.

One of the most reasonable explanations for social anxiety is that we are social beings and care about how others perceive us. A portion of this concern can be healthy. But, as the saying goes, everything in moderation. Unfortunately, for the millions of people suffering from social anxiety, this concern can reach unhealthy levels. They worry too much about being evaluated and lend too much importance to public performance.

Suki feared all kinds of social situations. She believed her parents' criticism and the bullying she received in high school to be responsible. At twenty-eight years old, she felt she'd experienced social anxiety symptoms all her life. In her first session, Suki shared her lifelong pattern of avoiding parties. Upon further exploration, Suki revealed her discomfort and avoidance of any social gatherings of three or more people. She found that she struggled with what to say, even in a one-on-one conversation. She felt she was terrible at small talk and was very uncomfortable with long pauses. She believed people were looking at her in judgment, maybe making fun of her behind her back, though she sensed this might be irrational. She was consistently afraid of embarrassing herself and of any potential social fallout as a result. Suki also feared her awkward behaviors would cause rejection. To prevent the possibility of any of the above, she mostly avoided engaging publicly, other than with a few childhood friends and her cousin. This avoidance, of course, encouraged more anxiety.

In her daily work at a graphic design company, Suki was forced to interact with coworkers. Though she had known them for some time, she still felt uncomfortable initiating conversation. Most at the office labeled her quiet. Suki believed her social anxiety held her back at work, as she had been passed over for promotion more than once. She rarely spoke up at meetings, fearing that others would notice her anxiety. On the romantic side, Suki had only been in one relationship, and this lasted just a few months. Her social fears frustrated her family, as she was anxious at family gatherings and sometimes avoided reunions and holiday celebrations. Suki even turned down her cousin's request that she be a bridesmaid in her wedding, due to fear of being a focal point of attention. Fortunately, Suki was now aware of these limitations and tired of their interference. She wanted more for her life. When she arrived in my office, she was ready to walk this path and got to work!

FEARS AND SYMPTOMS OF SOCIAL PHOBIA

* Intense anxiety in social situations with peers

* Fear that others will notice your anxiety

* Resistance to sharing your opinion

* Anticipatory anxiety over upcoming social gatherings

* Anxiety interacting with people in authority

* Fear of situations where you might be judged or criticized, like speaking in class

* Fear of being embarrassed or humiliated

* Constant worry that others are evaluating you

* Anxiety talking to strangers

* Anxiety speaking on the phone

* Fear of potentially embarrassing physical symptoms, like sweating, shaking, and blushing

* Avoidance of interactions or activities due to fear of humiliation

* Dread engaging in conversations

* Avoidance of circumstances where you could be the center of attention

* Harsh inner critic regarding social situations (spend a lot of time evaluating your comments following social interactions)

* Frequent assumptions about what others think of you

* Dread over posting on social media, spending an inordinate amount of time fretting over whether a post is "good enough," or being so anxious over

how it will be received that you avoiding posting at all

* Avoidance of commenting on other people's social media posts, even friends or family (though you may want to), for fear of being judged

BE SOCIABLE WITH EXPOSURE

As detailed in chapter 5, first identify all fears related to your social anxiety, then rank them according to the anxiety scale—zero being no anxiety, ten being a Tsunami of fear! Remember, the goal of exposure is to extinguish false fear messages via your brain's adaptation or desensitization. Do the work and you could soon be indifferent to the typical social events that once filled you with angst. The following exercises are the most effective exposures for social anxiety symptoms. Suki and countless others have committed to these and overcome their social anxiety! So you can, too! Of course, in a pandemic, choose exposures under each exercise that keeps you healthy, and wait on the rest!

Let's go...

1. **Play the exposure shame game:** Exposure exercises designed to encourage the possibility of criticism or judgment are extremely helpful. For example, you might want to wear a piece of clothing you wouldn't want to be caught dead in, like a funny hat or socks with questionable images. I recall seeing a man in his forties wearing a t-shirt with an image of toilet paper above a quote that read, "That's how I roll." Not sure if that was his shame game exposure or just his wardrobe of choice! At any

rate, it's a great example of exposure that encourages attention along with potential embarrassment for the socially anxious.

You could play the shame game with any behavior you believe could bring you conceivable unwanted attention. For example, you could ask a stranger for directions, even though you've got a GPS! This would be an exposure exercise if you fear criticism. Or you could listen to music, earbuds in, while singing loud enough for someone to hear you. Or you could speak on your cell phone while in line at the grocery store. Any of these will do. Suki practiced them all!

Some anxiety treatment experts suggest more extreme exposure to embarrassment or unwanted responses. For example, they might suggest you start screaming on a city street, or walk backwards on a crowded block, or even lay down and roll around while whining in the middle of a mall. I would not ask this of you, nor do I encourage anyone with social anxiety to act on these. Sure, these could be argued as flooding exposure. But in my over twenty years of doing this work, I have yet to see anybody with social phobia willing to do these extreme exposure exercises. So what good are they? Also, these actions don't reflect day-to-day healthy behavior. There's no point in encouraging unhealthy social behavior, when exposure is already necessary to achieve healthy or common social behavior. My focus in treating people with social anxiety is to encourage healthy behavior for an individual in the social world, in order to extinguish false fear messages. Therefore, when it comes to playing the exposure shame game, focus on behaviors that healthy, social people engage in on the regular.

2. **Ask questions.** This exposure takes two forms. First, practice asking others for logical assistance of some kind. For instance, you might ask staff in a grocery store where a particular item is located. Or you might ask a food server for more napkins. Or you might ask your bank teller for your current balance. Suki practiced occasionally asking coworkers for restaurant recommendations—and sometimes, just for an extra pen.

    Second, ask questions to engage people at social gatherings (and in general). Be sure to ask open-ended questions. Practice this with friends first, then take it out into the world! Start small. Then transition to asking questions in groups of three. Then ask questions at parties or social settings of any size. Be sincere. Ask not only what someone does for a living, but also about the specifics of their job. Ask what their hobbies are and what they've learned. Ask what they do on weekends. Ask about their families. Just be sure your questions can't be answered with a simple "yes" or "no." To add structure to this exposure, perhaps begin by asking two strangers a week one question each. Then maybe up the ante by asking acquaintances more personalized questions about their lives. Show interest. People love to talk about themselves. Ask and let them ramble. You'll be deemed a good listener—such a likeable, endearing feature! Suki advanced quickly with this exposure and she was elated with the results. She soon reported feeling far less social anxiety, and much to her surprise, people seemed excited to talk to her!

3. **Make contact.** Not just with your eyes. To start, smile and say "hello" to a stranger three times a week. Then increase that to once a day. Maybe greet a cashier, a Starbucks barista, people passing by who appear friendly, and so on.

4. **Make small talk.** Share a story from your own life or just share an opinion. It could be trivial or significant. Just add details. You don't have to be asked. Take initiative. These can be great conversation starters, especially at a party. Generally, people will listen, ask questions, and share a story or opinion of their own.

5. **Go dancing!** Most people with social anxiety feel very uncomfortable dancing, primarily because they fear being the center of attention. Secondly, because they fear being judged for their lack of ability. That's why dancing can be great exposure! So put on those dancing shoes and get out there! Maybe even show off a new move, as an added exposure exercise.

6. **Date.** (But only if single, of course. Infidelity is not an exposure strategy!). Build your confidence through this exposure exercise. Consider all dating to be practice. During dates, practice sharing aspects of your life. Also, ask questions! By the end of treatment, Suki had gone on a large number of dates and had a romantic interest that was developing.

7. **Take a class or volunteer.** Just participate. Practice raising your hand to answer questions or make comments. Start

gradually. Maybe begin with one question or comment per week. Focus on connecting with others via shared interests.

8. **Make phone calls.** Practice calling businesses to ask a question about a product. Practice phone conversations with family members and friends.

YOUR FALSE BELIEFS ARE NOT FRIENDLY

In addition to the above exposure exercises for social anxiety, the other key component in making your anxiety getaway, as always, is modifying the false beliefs that perpetuate your fears. There are several false beliefs I've seen consistently over the years that serve to maintain social anxiety. Take a look below for yours, then start practicing the reality-based corrections!

∗ **False Belief:** People are watching me and judging me all the time.

∗ **Reality-Based Belief:** If you imagine for a moment how immersed you are with how much is on your own plate, you can accurately apply this to others, too. We're all human beings. Most of us are absorbed with our own lives. We have our own agendas, plans, goals, thoughts, and feelings. Even when we do judge or criticize someone, it is through our own prism. We are judging based on our own perspectives, according to our own struggles. The judgments and criticisms that do arise have little to do with the person on the receiving end. In other words, people aren't considering you a fraction as much as you think. Frankly, this is because most people don't care that much about you on a moment-to-moment basis. And not from a selfish standpoint—they're just too wrapped up in their own struggles.

* **False Belief:** It's of absolute importance that people think well of me.

* **Reality-Based Belief:** We are social beings, so it's healthy to care about what others think. Only sociopaths seem to lack care or concern about how they're perceived by others. And yet, even they want friends to like them. Face it: we are a world built on social interaction. But, it's only healthy to care about what other people think of you in small doses. In fact, you're far healthier the *less* you care about what other people think. That doesn't mean, however, that you should act in ways that are dismissive and disrespectful. It means you care less about their opinions of your own worth, personal choices, and who they think you are. This is your life. It's healthy to do what you think is best (as long as that is indeed healthy!). To make choices based on your own path and not anyone else's. It's up to you.

The main foundation of social anxiety is the elevation of others through comparison and the belief that what they think of you deeply matters. This false perspective considers others superior, thereby making you inferior! The fact is, we're all human beings! No one is better than any other person. Sure, some people have strengths that are widely accepted or even celebrated by our culture. And maybe this provides them with lots of finances, or lots of attention. Still, it doesn't make them better than anybody else. It just means our culture values what they're offering, whether valid or not. We are all just people. It's always an error (and a false belief) to consider others to be more important or special than anyone else.

And no one lives life unscathed. We don't know what goes on behind closed doors with other people. We all have our foibles, ups and downs, and struggles. No one is more special than another, despite what our society suggests by way of status, profession, or popularity!

* **False Belief:** I can't handle being embarrassed. I'll die.

* **Reality-Based Belief:** You've felt embarrassed before. And yet, here you sit! Clearly, you can handle it better than you think.

Also, you are blowing out of proportion situations as embarrassing, when few others deem them to be. For example, a pause in conversation can trigger high anxiety for social phobics. But it's barely a blip on the radar for those who don't struggle in this area. And even when truly in universally embarrassing situations, others have clearly survived them and moved on.

* **False Belief:** I'm no good at small talk.

* **Reality-Based Belief:** There are people who are great small talkers. They tend to be more on the extroverted side, telling stories of minutiae and being entertaining while doing so. And that's great for some. Conversely, there are people who don't naturally come with the gift of gab. But they can improve! With just a little exposure and the modification of false beliefs, you, too, could be a small talk natural. Anyone can improve this skill. The very nature of small talk lacks pressure to engage in a meaningful way. So practice skimming the surface. The point is just to engage people in a sincere manner.

* **False Belief:** I'm not confident enough to talk to people and work through my social anxiety.

* **Reality-Based Belief:** Confidence isn't necessarily required to talk to people. For instance, there are plenty of insecure people who are social butterflies! The fact is, real confidence is earned. It's not inadvertent. It doesn't just arrive someday. To gain confidence socially, one must be social. It's only logical. As usual, it's about facing fear and earning confidence. You can't expect to feel more confident without challenging fear and engaging repeatedly in social settings that build confidence.

* **False Belief:** I hate parties.

* **Reality-Based Belief:** When people struggle with anxiety, they come up with all sorts of excuses to avoid what they fear. One of the most frequent excuses is to tell yourself you dislike an activity, situation, environment, or experience. Social anxiety often leads one to practice the belief that they hate parties, even while having a sense that they're not being honest with themselves or others. Meanwhile, as mentioned earlier, fearing and hating something are two different matters. Following successful anxiety treatment, you can attend parties without fear (even though they still may not be your passion)!

Don't forget, all phobias can be resolved if you engage your exposures and adopt reality-based beliefs! So, wait no longer. Go make your anxiety getaway!

CHAPTER 9

I HEAR YE OCD, BUT
I'M NOT LISTENING

"Rather than being your thoughts and emotions, be the awareness behind them."

—Eckhart Tolle

"The best way out is always through."

—Robert Frost

"Obsess much?"

—Unknown teenager heard talking to a friend

Entire books have been written on the subject of obsessive-compulsive disorder (OCD) alone, many of them with interesting details addressing its neurobiological underpinnings. In other words, they detail brain stuff focused on OCD's location and communication mishaps when it comes to processing and letting go of "disturbing" thoughts. This "brain" focus moves way beyond what I describe in chapter 3 on anxiety syndromes in general. So because there are so many books pertaining to the neurobiology of OCD, I've done away with further brain highlights on this subject. Instead, to continue attending to a quick and effective anxiety getaway, I've focused only on what you need to know to manage OCD symptoms and claim your calm. Just remember that at the end of the day, like all anxiety issues, OCD is about fear!

What's most important to know initially is that OCD is a neurobiological syndrome (literally part of one's brain) that prevents some thoughts from processing correctly, causing them, for lack of a better phrase, to "get stuck." Those with OCD are born with this syndrome, whether it decides to make a big dramatic entrance in childhood or wait until adulthood.

For those adults unaware of their latent OCD—other than minor early indicators that family members have always described as "quirky"—OCD can explode in times of stress or even times of great change (most change, whether positive or negative, is stressful).

In fact, many do not experience symptoms that interfere with their daily lives until they go through a stressful life event. Examples of stressful events that often trigger the launch of OCD's symptoms include a major illness, a trauma or an accident, childbirth, parenting a newborn (often called "postpartum OCD"), and many more. With a major stressor, OCD can truly detonate and create the impression that it "came out of nowhere."

When it does decide to come out of the shadows and introduce itself, OCD can feel like a wave of terror, typically leaving the formerly "OCD-free" individual in an anxiety tailspin.

The common analogy of our brains as super computers with a multitude of functions and amazing feats comes to mind. However, like any old MacBook, brains can have glitches, too! For when it comes to the human brain, there seems to be no shortage of possible "malfunctions," such as schizophrenia, epilepsy, ADHD, Tourette's, bipolar disorder, and so on. These glitches are there to stay, and there's little one can do other than manage the symptoms. This is true for OCD, too. This, in essence, makes it a little different than a phobia or struggle with panic attacks. And though this is a reality that all with OCD must come to terms with, there is something very positive (and, more importantly, reality-based!) that makes it differ from most other brain glitches. And that is...drum roll, please...OCD does not have to lead to any real suffering once you treat yourself with exposure and false belief modification! Following successful treatment, if you meet any new symptoms with reality-based beliefs and exposure exercises when needed, your OCD can be nothing more than an occasional nuisance to be dealt with. Similar to other ailments with which people contend.

If you follow my instructions in this chapter (and refresh your memory with chapters 5 and 6, as needed), you'll know just what to do to become your OCD's master, so your OCD doesn't master you!

A LITTLE OCD?

OCD is a common disorder and a commonly misunderstood one. Still, public awareness has grown, with many books written on the subject and depictions in entertainment (both comedy and drama). I'd like to think the two seasons of A&E's docuseries *Obsessed* that I participated in as an anxiety specialist, treating many of the show's participants struggling with OCD, had an impact, as well. I know I considered it a public service.

Unfortunately, OCD still remains misunderstood by most of the population. For example, people love to say, "Sorry, I'm a little OCD," when it comes to their perfectionistic tendencies. Helpful life management habits do not suggest OCD. And you can't be a little OCD—you either have it or you don't! Just like you can't be a little bit pregnant. This, of course, doesn't mean there isn't a range of OCD expression, from severe to lesser forms. This is true for almost every ailment or syndrome, I suppose.

But no matter the difference in degree, there are shared symptoms in all conditions. This is even true for the common cold. For example, with a cold, just about everybody has a runny nose. For some, it might feel like it's marathon-length runny. Yet for others, it's just a 5K.

Before we discuss OCD any further, to make your anxiety getaway, it's important to address what it entails and how its symptoms manifest.

WHAT IS OCD, REALLY?

Though false belief (at it again!) is at the root of OCD symptom trouble, the "spark" is a thought that has become stuck. These thoughts are rarely focused on real-life issues that most are concerned with, like job security or relationship conflict (though they can be). OCD's focus tends to be on fear-inducing thoughts that are completely illogical, unlikely, or extreme.

For instance, Kevin had an obsessive fear of flooding the house if he were to accidentally leave the bathroom faucet running. Though he could see no water flowing when he'd check, his brain continued to tell him the faucets could be "on" and that he was in danger of setting off a bathroom tsunami.

Another former patient, Isabella, had repeated, unwanted thoughts about planet Earth hurtling through space. Morning, noon, and night, she struggled with crippling anxiety over how this occurred and why.

The above examples depict what I've already described as the classic "brain stuck" symptom of OCD. It's not that these thoughts are thoughts no one else has had. Typically, all OCD-linked thoughts are thoughts everyone has had at one point or another. But when it comes to an obsession, the offending thought becomes lodged in the OCD-sticky brain and doesn't process in a manner that naturally lets it go. Of course, preceding this sticky situation is a belief that the thought is somehow a meaningful warning of danger, followed by a battle to avoid it. This is what truly sets the obsession in motion.

Even if there is some awareness of the irrationality of the obsessive thought, when a thought continues no matter the confirmation of its wackiness from the environment or experience, it can be a challenge to simply let it go. For instance, if someone were to repeatedly whisper the same phrase into your ear, it would be difficult not to listen. Here, that someone is your brain. This is where treatment is needed.

When someone comes to my center for help with OCD, whether aware of their diagnosis or not, the cognitive side of OCD is often shared first. This is because, although OCD can come with a host of compulsive behaviors, it is the thoughts that most are concerned about. These thoughts often have themes most would describe as upsetting, with some perceived as "shameful." Unfortunately, this factor can encourage many to suffer silently without seeking help. There's no need for this! OCD isn't personal, though it certainly can feel that way (remember, feelings aren't facts).

Moving on, when considering OCD, there are two major components: obsessions and compulsions. **Obsessions** are not what most people think they are. The terms "obsessed" and "obsessions" have become a part of the vernacular. Many frequently say they're "obsessed" with this or that in daily conversations. However, what they're driving at is a feeling of passion for something.

A true "obsession" is an intrusive, unwanted, recurring thought, image, or impulse that is considered to be inappropriate or irrational, and causes some degree of suffering. As said, obsessions are not typical concerns over stress in relationships or careers. They can manifest around many different topics, but some common obsessions are fear of germs, fear of causing others harm (stabbing someone, hitting someone with your car) or of harm coming to oneself, inappropriate sexual thoughts (e.g., incest), violent images, numbers, and more.

The other OCD hallmark is compulsive behavior meant to undo a specific obsession or anxiety. **Compulsions** are defined as repetitive behaviors or rituals (physical or mental) that one engages in to escape obsessive fear. These behaviors can interfere with daily life, due to their time-consuming nature and frustrating disruption.

There is a large range of compulsive behaviors, such as cleaning, checking, ordering, and washing. To cope with his obsession of flooding the house, Kevin checked the faucet by tapping the handle ten times in a row (or until he felt okay). To cope with her Earth-hurtling-through-space fear, Isabella frequently planted her feet on the floor in a heavy stance.

Mental compulsions include repetitive mental acts designed to counter the anxiety evoked by a disturbing thought, image, or impulse. These include praying, repeating various phrases, and counting.

Oftentimes, but not always, compulsions are clearly attached to a specific obsession. Unfortunately, though compulsions are designed by an individual to reduce anxiety in the short run (they're avoidant, and by now you know what that means!), they actually create and maintain more anxiety in the long run (exactly!). Reducing compulsive avoidance behavior is a key to claiming your calm from OCD and making your anxiety getaway!

Obsessions and compulsions are intertwined. As was just established, obsessions are repetitive thoughts that are unreasonable, disturbing in nature, and difficult to stop. Compulsions are behaviors or mental rituals designed to reduce anxiety caused by obsessions. Remember, trying to think less of a fearful thought actually causes you to think it more by creating false fear messages. When you fight an obsession via the avoidance maneuver of compulsive behavior, it creates a feedback loop that further solidifies the obsession. What you resist, persists! And compulsions are resistant behaviors, whether mental or physical.

For example, a patient named Jack developed a Satan obsession and was terrified. Though he hadn't participated in organized religion in years, he still had a connection to his family's devout upbringing. In his first session, Jack described how a thought of loving and admiring Satan entered his head while watching a horror movie ("The one with the scary looking, possessed nun," he said.). Upon evaluation, it appeared that Jack was a compassionate individual who had no interest in hurting anybody. Yet, he equated his obsession with Satan to mean that he was evil himself—sort of a "like attracts like" theory!

To cope, Jack began avoiding anything that reminded him of the devil. For example, he avoided the color red as much as possible. Stop signs and traffic signals were unavoidable, and thus made him anxious. Though he used to listen to a lot of heavy metal, he curtailed this completely, fearful that he'd hear a song about the devil (the subject of almost one out of every ten metal tunes!). He also stopped watching horror movies, though they were his favorites. And anytime he observed the number six in a text message or cell phone number, it triggered anxiety, too. Subsequently, he resisted returning these messages. For instance, his sister's number contained two sixes. She was not happy with the shun.

Jack's avoidance served to encourage his obsession. But he also engaged in compulsive behaviors that reinforced his obsession even further. For example, he'd repeat the phrase, "I am holy," every time he had an obsessive thought about love for the devil. He also soon started placing his hands in a prayer position when struck by these thoughts. As described above, this was the OCD feedback loop in action.

COMMON FEARS AND SYMPTOMS OF OCD

If you can name it, we humans can fear it. For the individual with OCD, his or her obsessions can contain just about any subject. However, if you were to take a cross-section of those with OCD throughout much of the world, you'd find that no matter their ethnicity, culture, socioeconomic status, or childhood history, there are common obsessions shared by most (negating any idea of a deep-seated meaning behind them). Why is this? Because there are universally disturbing realities in life that cut across differences, such as loss, murder, pedophilia, mental illness, social rejection, abandonment, medical illness, accidents, lack of control, and more that can impact many. Most people don't want to entertain these themes. For someone with untreated OCD, when a thought with any of these themes occurs and they fight it due to its unpleasant nature, they're setting themselves up for an obsession. The more they fight it, the more it becomes a stranglehold. As you've now learned, this battle teaches the brain that what you're fighting is "dangerous." Subsequently, false fear messages commence, trying to protect you from the thought itself and its theme's specific environmental anxiety triggers.

Here is a list of the most common fears and symptoms addressed in OCD treatment (not in any order). This is in no way an exhaustive list (as said, we can fear anything), just a list of the most frequently seen. Here we go...

* Unwanted thoughts one deems weird, terrible, malicious or nonsensical

* Obsessive fears over dirt, germs, toxins, contaminants, fecal matter, other bodily waste, or house cleaning products

* Excessive hand washing, showering, and grooming rituals

* Repeating neutral actions a specific number of times or until it feels right (rising from a chair, turning off a light switch, locking a door, taking a step, walking through doorways, opening a cabinet, etc.)

* Excessive house cleaning

* Associating neutral concepts, objects, or images with "bad" events or the possibility of them occurring (songs, clothing, colors, numbers, etc.)

* Obsessive fears about body odor, appearance, or functioning

* Hyper-focus on right and wrong

* Hyper-concern with losing something of value or leaving it behind (phone, jewelry, etc.)

* Obsessive fears about contracting an illness (MS, cancer, blood clots, tumors, etc.)

* Fear you'll say or do something awful, embarrassing, or out of your control

* Hyper-concern with objects being in the "off" or safety position at home (locks, stove, windows, faucets, etc.), especially when leaving

* Often seeking reassurance from loved ones that all will be okay, or that a specific behavior or statement wasn't harmful

* Fear of saying or doing something wrong that will lead to harm, punishment, or negative consequences to self or family members

* Obsessive fear of being gay, though one is heterosexual

* Obsessive fear of harm coming to a loved one

* Over-concern with "bad" events occurring (spouse or children being kidnapped, fire, burglary, home invasion, flooding of the house, etc.)

* Fear of impulsively harming someone (stabbing someone, hitting someone with car, etc.)

* Fear of impulsively hurting oneself (jumping off a bridge, driving or stepping into oncoming traffic, etc.)

* Recurring unwanted thoughts of death or violent images one deems inappropriate or unacceptable (beheadings, shootings, etc.)

* Recurring unwanted sexual thoughts one deems inappropriate or unacceptable (pedophilia, bestiality, etc.)

* Recurring unwanted religious thoughts one deems inappropriate or unacceptable

* Difficulty tolerating sounds that most ignore (someone's chewing, breathing, etc.).

* Counting items unnecessarily or as a mental ritual

* Repeated checking of tasks or other items to ensure they've been managed correctly

* Superstitious fears (touching an object will cause a bad event to happen, etc.)

* Hyper-frequency of ordering or arranging objects

* Re-reading excerpts or sentences repeatedly

* Mentally repeating phrases

Whew! That's a long list of common symptoms. Most people with OCD struggle with at least three of these. Thankfully for the OCD sufferer, there is anxiety relief to be found!

I THINK, THEREFORE I SPAM

As already defined, obsessions are unwanted thoughts one cannot seem to stop thinking (even with the awareness they're irrational) that encourage anxiety and upset. But thoughts are not inherently powerful on their own. Thoughts are just thoughts. Our brain is designed to think, so it does. And oftentimes, arriving like unwanted and uninvited spam (the messages, not the faux ham), our thinking is caught up in wasteful, non-task-oriented thoughts that are meaningless at best, and self-defeating at worst. But thoughts can't make something happen independently. In reality, thinking something won't make it happen (despite what some believe, there is no real evidence to the contrary). Thoughts are given the labels we assign them based on the belief they're either a "good" or "bad" thought.

But, again, our thoughts themselves don't have much power at all. In fact, they don't have any, other than the power we give them.

Why *do* we give our thoughts so much power to affect us, then? Is it that we assume they're personal in nature because they emanate from our brain? Isn't thinking just what our brains do, and what they're supposed to do? No matter whether our thoughts are meaningless, silly, task-oriented, intellectual, funny, or horror-driven, our brains still think them. In reality, thoughts are just thoughts. No more, no less. It's best to think of most thoughts as brain emissions. And thoughts are largely neutral, regardless of the value you give them or the category to which you assign them. What is meaningful is if you respond to them with belief, and follow that with action. Remember our beliefs, not our thoughts, inform our choices. For example, most people would say it's wrong to kill your neighbor. But as numerous

Dateline episodes have shown, many have believed this to be a splendid idea (at least at the time).

It's easy to believe that thoughts alone can create anxiety when many are considered to be universally disturbing. These, combined with the stickiness of the OCD brain (to be clear, just one small part of the brain), can make for an unpleasant experience. But, as is always the case, it's your belief about a thought that makes it bad or good. So, if you label a thought "bad" or some derivate thereof, such as "dangerous," "shameful," "inappropriate," or "evil," the result is obvious. You'll be anxious! Labeling thoughts this way primes the pump for an OCD obsession. So again, it's all about belief. That said, it's not easy to see repetitive, unwanted thoughts (obsessions) of pedophilia, murder, suicide, contamination, loss of control, harm coming to loved ones, illness, and a host of others as neutral (though this is an important practice to start now!). When thoughts like those above become stuck in your brain on repeat, playing the same note again and again and again, the question of "What if...?" can cause terror.

It's often "What If" thoughts that are the obsessive cornerstone of OCD suffering. And when struggling with the aforementioned fears and symptoms, they're also a common indicator that you have OCD. For example, Shawna suffered from intense obsessions of stabbing her husband. At times, she feared it even felt like a desired impulse. These terrified her to her core, as she loved her husband very much and had never physically hurt anyone in her life. Yet this obsession plagued her. Its most common form was, "Even though I don't want to, what if I lose control and stab my husband?" Images of her husband's blood-soaked face caused by the protruding knife Shawna had plunged into his forehead entered her mind at the most inopportune times. To cope, she hid the knives away in a closet, only saving a butter knife. Yet the thoughts continued to torture her, especially in quiet moments, like when she slept beside her husband or watched TV. Again, though she knew it was silly, she couldn't stop the thought, because... "What if?"

Anxiety Getaway Tip

When thoughts begin with "What If," it's a good indicator your OCD is talking, so don't listen to it! Practice identifying thoughts as just thoughts. It's your beliefs and actions that matter.

The struggle with "What If" thoughts speaks to a foundational issue of OCD—the difficulty tolerating uncertainty. Most OCD sufferers (and phobia and panic sufferers, too) crave certainty associated with their particular struggle and beyond. Most want to *know* that nothing will go wrong, that their fearful thought is not true or will never, ever, ever happen. But complete certainty is hard to find almost anywhere in life. Almost nothing is 100 percent certain! For example, back to Shawna: the chances were so incredibly slim that she would lose control and impulsively stab her husband. Why? Because acting out impulsively, violently, and criminally was not part of her history. The best predictor of future human behavior is past behavior. Even Shawna herself, when asked, said she didn't really *believe* she would commit such an act. However, she still deeply disliked lacking the complete certainty that she would never lose control and commit such a horrible act. Even 99.9 percent certainty was not enough! After all, she knew others in the world had done so. She had seen it on the news and in many episodes of *Law and Order*!

When she could no longer sleep for fear of acting on her obsession, she knew she needed help. As you might imagine, her husband was totally on board! Soon after Shawna arrived at my office and shared her story, we addressed the need to practice identifying thoughts as just thoughts. And the need to practice accepting the fact that though there is never 100 percent certainty for almost anything, she could live with 99.9 percent or even less! Next, because ultimately resolving OCD's obsessions is about exposure and correcting false beliefs, we got down to business.

KEEP YOUR COMPOSURE WITH OCD EXPOSURE

Remember, to extinguish any OCD obsessions (as with all false fear messages), you must *face* fear without avoidance. To overcome anxiety caused by obsessions, you'll engage in all that is detailed in chapter 5, so return to it as often as needed. However, when it comes to obsessional anxiety, there are some special exposure matters to think about. So below, I've included key exposure considerations for all your obsessional anxiety getaway needs. It's time to unstick some stuck thoughts!

Let's go!

1. Just like with phobias, obsessions usually manifest in the avoidance of objects, events, and situations in the environment. So again, as detailed in chapter 5, your exposure must involve gradually facing items on your written anxiety trigger list. For example, Jack's Satan obsession manifested in numerous fears. To manage his terror, he began with exposure assignments that

triggered no more than a three on the anxiety scale. His first assignment was to watch a comedy movie about the devil. He noted that certain scenes sparked his anxiety more than others. We then identified these scenes and added them to the list of exposure items to address gradually. For instance, he was terrified of scenes that involved punishing people in hell. Next, further up the list in anxiety difficulty was listening to songs about the devil. As a heavy metal fan, he knew many that triggered anxiety ("Runnin' With The Devil" by Van Halen and Judas Priest's "Devil's Child," for starters). He was to listen to both once a day.

Other assignments included:

* Placing a devil image on his iPhone wallpaper

* Writing the number six in groups of three over and over again (666)

* Drawing a picture of the devil as he saw it

* Wearing a red shirt

* Writing the phrases "I love the devil" and "I am evil" ten times a day

Jack was diligent and completed all his exposure exercises. As is typical, the smaller fears on his anxiety trigger list required less exposure time to adapt to than his larger fears. For instance, his brain grew desensitized to the iPhone wallpaper exposure after a total of just a couple of hours. He was relieved once he finished facing all of the exposures on his list, and happily free from any devilish anxiety!

Shawna committed to exposure quickly, due to her intense desire to extinguish her obsessive fear of stabbing her husband. One of her more challenging assignments was to hold a butcher knife for thirty minutes a day while her husband was in another room. As for her most difficult assignment, for ten days, Shawna left a sharp knife under the bed while she and her husband slept. These initially filled Shawna with such extreme anxiety that she panicked. Once she completed about seventeen hours of each, she no longer feared either. Soon, she graduated to refilling the kitchen drawers with their knife set and was no longer plagued by this obsession. Her brain had adapted. She achieved her anxiety getaway!

2. When it comes to your self-help OCD treatment, you must also add the extra exposure element of ceasing any compulsions. Remember, your compulsions are the behaviors or mental rituals you perform to reduce the anxiety associated with your obsessions. You'll need to consider your work on reducing and removing them as a large part of your exposure work itself. Why? Because these are the equivalent of avoidance and, as you've learned, this resistance against anxiety only serves to maintain and encourage more! So if you're still performing your compulsions while engaging in exposure, know that you're undoing progress (and only adding to your anxious OCD suffering).

Anxiety Getaway Tip

Some OCD sufferers only struggle with obsessions (called Pure-O) and do not have compulsions. If this is true for you, then focus solely on exposure to obsessions and skip this next compulsion management step.

There are several compulsion management strategies with which to conduct OCD exposure. You might not need to apply them all.

Take a look below to determine which compulsion controls apply to your particular struggle. Then add that compulsion's management to your anxiety triggers list.

a. Reduce the number of times you perform a specific compulsion until you're down to one or none, depending on whether there is any rational component to your compulsion. For example, checking a door lock is necessary—once! Walking backward and forward seven times through every doorway is never rational—not even once!

Keep in mind that immediately removing a compulsive behavior will increase your anxiety. Remember, these were created to cope with your obsessive fear, so doing this will be more of a flooding experience. If you're ready, go for it. You'll just be sitting with a high degree of anxiety until your brain adapts to the degree of obsessive fear associated with that compulsion.

Still, just as with other anxiety triggers on your list (of which reducing compulsions will be one), it's easiest to do this work gradually, if that's an option. Rather than flooding, you can slowly reduce the number of compulsions you perform. When your brain adapts to a certain number, reduce it further until it's gone!

For example, reducing a stove checking compulsion from twenty times to fifteen might bring your anxiety to a three on the anxiety scale, as opposed to an eight on the anxiety scale if too quickly reduced to checking ten times. Start with fifteen, then. This would be gradual exposure.

As usual, go at your own pace. Again, move toward reducing your compulsion to one, when it's appropriate. Otherwise, work toward zero. For instance, there's no rational need to tap a faucet a specific number of times once you've turned it off.

b. Another method for removing compulsions gradually is to reduce time spent on them. Some compulsions are performed for a length of time (or until it feels right), as opposed to a specific number of times. These can include hand washing, showering, grooming rituals, and more. As I directed with reducing numbered compulsions, you'll do the same here with time. For example, those with contamination fears would gradually reduce the length of hand washing time per sink visit, with a focus on a rational, healthy maximum.

c. A third compulsion removal method is flooding, as referenced earlier. Sorry, but sometimes with compulsions, this is just necessary. It's what I call the "stop doing that now" strategy (not a very fancy name,

I admit). For example, every morning, Ethan had an obsession that harm might befall his family that day. So each morning while starting his car, Ethan would repeat to himself, "Raisins are dried grapes." Just another example of the nonsensical nature of OCD. Somehow, he associated this phrase with protection for his family. And it was this compulsion that he needed to stop to encourage his brain to adapt to his obsession, so it no longer produced these false fear messages.

Remember Isabella's compulsion of planting her feet in a heavy stance in response to her hurtling-Earth obsession? One major exposure assignment was for her to stop herself from performing this action. Specifically, whenever she felt compelled, she was to immediately walk away. Even at home. Soon enough, this compulsion interfered no more. She was close to fully extinguishing her obsession, with just a couple more assignments to face.

3. When it comes to OCD symptom exposure, don't forget to also engage in exposure to your obsessive thoughts themselves. How? With imaginal exposure, of course! Again, if you need a full refresher, return to chapter 5.

   I instructed Shawna to write a story of her worst fear realized. As a reminder, this is a detailed first-person, present-tense narrative. Surprisingly, Shawna did not enjoy this. Go figure!

   Shawna started her story by describing her anxiety while she laid in bed beside her husband. With vivid style, she then shared feeling the impulse build until she couldn't control it anymore. Her graphic story depicted her pulling a butcher knife from under her pillow and stabbing her husband repeatedly, blood splattering on the bedroom walls. It ended with her alone in prison. Her life, as she knew it, over. As is common, Shawna cried repeatedly as she wrote and then read this story for exposure. Soon, however, she could read it without any anxiety. Her obsession was dissipating.

As another imaginal exposure strategy, don't forget to use your imagination (obviously) to take your obsessive thought to its ultimate extreme. For example, I directed Isabella to purposely imagine herself standing on planet Earth while it sped throughout the galaxy. I even had her imagine our planet hurtling through space so out of control that it spun at warp speed. It couldn't get more ridiculous. And that's the point! When you take your obsessive thoughts as far as they can go, your anxiety has no room to breathe. You're sucking the air right out of it.

4. Remember, seventeen hours is the average length of exposure time your brain needs to extinguish fear for each anxiety trigger on your list (some might take far less). With OCD, your focus is on desensitizing your brain to your obsessions. Consider exposure as bad tasting medicine for that process. Just keep chipping away on the path to your anxiety getaway!

Anxiety Getaway Tip

Don't make the mistake of thinking about your OCD obsessions differently than you would any fear I've described in this book. At the end of the day, we're still talking about facing fear.

Some new to exposure believe that it sounds self-punishing and negative, especially when one considers encouraging the more commonly disturbing obsessions. And I understand. If you were to describe exposure to the average person on the street, many would think you're crazy for entertaining it. Most people would avoid exposure (especially imaginal) without understanding its scientifically proven effectiveness. It does sound negative, being encouraged to sit in seventeen hours of fear (perhaps many times). But things are often not what they seem. False fear messages, anyone? Sure, positive thinking has some benefits. But our culture tends to perpetuate a false narrative regarding the degree of benefits of positive thinking. Positive thinking only takes you so far. It certainly will not help you overcome fear (though it can give you extra inspiration for your exposure assignments). It's the action of exposure that's necessary, not positive thinking. In fact, it's been shown that a positive thinking practice can actually inspire negative thinking. Why? Because there is no positive without the negative. The more you keep trying to force positive thoughts, the more you encourage negative thoughts. Remember, what you resist, persists! It's always better to focus on reality-based beliefs. And the reality is that exposure works. Now that's a positive!

Some fear that purposely thinking uncomfortable thoughts will cause them to occur in life. But as already established, we're not that powerful. Thoughts alone cannot cause an external event. I'm currently thinking of pigs flying past my office window and I'm pretty sure that won't happen. As far as mentally encouraging your worst fear, the truth is that you're already thinking these thoughts, anyway. These are the obsessions you've been fighting. In other words, with exposure, I'm not prescribing a thought you're not already thinking!

And with your self-directed exposure, you'll turn the tables on OCD by prescribing yourself the very thoughts and situations you've been avoiding. This is how we overcome fear! You train your brain to adapt by feeding it the very stimulus or subject matter you're afraid of, until it is desensitized. This is what exposure is all about.

You must purposely think the thought you don't want to think. You must purposely invite those "What If" thoughts. To truly overcome an OCD obsession, one must face it. You must look it in the eye! No one has ever successfully faced fear by running from it or trying to pretend it's not there. Or by talking about its possible origins. You can't go around it, under it, or over it, either. You've got to go through it!

OCD HEAD GAMES

With OCD, one can obsess about anything, so a specific belief isn't always easy to determine.

But why is it that only disturbing, uncomfortable thoughts get stuck in one's OCD brain? Why don't positive thoughts get stuck? Because of belief! Because we believe it would be bad or dangerous for whatever we're thinking to come to fruition. Or we've labeled the thought itself as "bad" or "inappropriate." Without this belief, you wouldn't struggle with obsessional anxiety. So in addition to the need for exposure to desensitize you to your brain's false fear messages, false belief modification is essential, too (return to chapter 6 for a refresher, as needed).

It's time to get real about your beliefs and OCD. Beliefs will inform your choices and experiences when it comes to responding to OCD symptoms, as they do with any anxiety struggle. Transitioning from false beliefs to reality-based beliefs changes the way you behave and respond. So review the false beliefs and their accompanying reality-based beliefs below to continue your practice (as detailed in chapter 6) by applying them to your OCD!

∗ **False Belief**: I can control my thoughts.

∗ **Reality-Based Belief**: You cannot. One bit of evidence is that you don't know what you'll be thinking ten minutes from now. However, you can control how you respond to your thoughts.

∗ **False Belief**: I am defined by my OCD.

∗ **Reality-Based Belief**: You have OCD. It's a small part of your brain. It's not who you are. Most people have some challenges. It comes with being human. This might be yours.

∗ **False Belief**: I must be evil or a bad person for having this thought.

∗ **Reality-Based Belief**: No one is considered evil or bad for having thoughts alone. Think about people in history that have been described as "bad" or "evil." The descriptor is based on their behaviors. Thoughts in and of themselves don't make someone "bad" or "evil." Horror writers (like Stephen King) can make a living from thoughts most would label inappropriate, at best. To commit so much time and effort to these thoughts equates to a willingness to indulge them. So, most horror writers must know that these are just thoughts. They don't reflect their character.

* **False Belief**: Sometimes my OCD doesn't bother me as much. I think that means it's getting better on its own. Looks like I don't have to do any exposure.

* **Reality-Based Belief**: OCD obsessions can wax and wane. In other words, sometimes they're better, sometimes they're worse. Without treatment, your anxious suffering will continue when caught up in obsessions and compulsions. You've got to do the work to free yourself from OCD's grasp.

* **False Belief**: I can't handle my OCD symptoms. This is too difficult. I'll probably suffer with these for the rest of my life.

* **Reality-Based Belief**: Though it is a challenge, you choose the suffering. You can handle far more than you think. And you can choose to handle your symptoms in a healthy manner with the strategies in this book. So choose this now. Do your exposure, modify your false beliefs, and claim your calm. It's up to you.

* **False Belief**: Obsessions are disturbing because they're *my* thoughts.

* **Reality-Based Belief**: Accepting the truth that most of our thoughts aren't personal and are simply a byproduct of the brain's function goes a long way when managing OCD. And where is the proof that these are your thoughts? Especially after having heard about the subject matter elsewhere? The brain is designed to think. So why not let it think without attaching value or

judgment to thoughts? This can be your practice, especially with thoughts that are clearly irrational.

* **False Belief**: Because I'm having thoughts about _____ (insert your feared, so-called "inappropriate" thought here), it means I want to indulge a desire.

* **Reality-Based Belief**: We are not bothered by thoughts that are aligned with who we are or what we want. In fact, when congruent, they usually sound good to us! So know that when you have an obsessive thought, any upset feeling or discomfort toward it is an indicator that it's just OCD, not your true interest.

* **False Belief**: My thoughts disturb me.

* **Reality-Based Belief**: It's the belief about a thought that is doing the disturbing. Again, thoughts are just thoughts. However, if you label a thought with the belief that it's "bad" (or some similar judgmental value), it can become stuck. This is OCD's bread and butter!

Though OCD has its challenges, remember that fear is fear! And freedom from suffering is your choice. Face your false fear messages with exposure, modify those false beliefs, and make your obsessional anxiety getaway!

CONCLUSION

Taking action to overcome anxiety can be one of the most profound experiences of your life. Not only is it an investment in *you*, but as you reach your goals, it can provide an ultra-satisfying burst of newfound freedom and confidence. And so much more! That's the beauty of the anxiety treatment in this book—it has far-reaching effects.

Making progress just takes a mix of motivation and commitment. You *can* move beyond fear and anxiety. It can be done. You're stronger than you think.

With this book, you have taken a major step toward claiming your calm. Now it's time to implement all that you've learned in the course of your reading. So carry on. Even when it feels like you've reached the darkest point with your anxiety, you're so close to being free. The more you allow yourself to feel anxiety's discomfort, the closer you are to liberation. Just keep going. Inch by inch. Step by step. And you will soon prevail. You will soon outsmart the false fear messages that plague your brain.

In these pages, I've provided all that is needed to overcome your anxiety symptoms. Now it's up to you. However, though this is a self-help book, you don't have to go at it alone. Everyone needs a helping hand sometimes. And if it's an expert one, even better! So if need be, don't hesitate to contact my anxiety treatment center via KickFear.com, or an anxiety treatment expert in your area, for assistance.

This marks the end of this book, but an auspicious beginning for you. I wish you all the best on this life-changing adventure. You are on your way to what I hope is an extended, here-to-stay, anxiety getaway.

ACKNOWLEDGMENTS

First, I want to acknowledge the teachers I've had along the way. Many thanks to my peers, professors, and mentors. And to my patients, who have taught me so much about anxiety and fear through their own struggles.

Thanks also to the colleagues, psychiatrists, and medical doctors who continue to entrust me with treating their patients' anxiety symptoms.

A heartfelt thanks to everyone at Mango for the opportunity and their fantastic work in the service of this book. A special, sincere thanks to my editor, Natasha Vera, for her insightful and adept feedback throughout the course of my writing. And an extra thanks for giving me the freedom to write from interest and passion, not solely know-how and experience.

To friends and family, I am grateful for their love and care. Most specifically, thanks to my sister for her unconditional love. It always means so much to know her ear is there to bend, should I need to bend it! Her sweet laugh always makes what ails a lot better.

To Todd, my brother-in-arms, whose texts and voicemail messages of love and support were much appreciated during the course of writing this book. I'm forever grateful for his friendship over the last thirty-five years, the talks, his open-mindedness, and as always, the laughs.

To my loves, Sam and Penny.

And most importantly to my wife, whose love, intelligence, wisdom, kindness, and compassion have meant the world to me and my development as an individual (and a professional). Thank you for giving me all the time needed to write, sacrificing many chats and weekends, and not judging when I walked around like a zombie muttering to myself during late night writing breaks. Her unwavering belief and never-ending support were appreciated beyond measure. I couldn't have done it without her. I have no words to express my love, admiration, and respect. Thanks for...everything.

NOTES

Chapter 3: Your Brain on Anxiety

1.) World Economic Forum. "This is the World's Biggest Mental Health Problem—and You Might Not Have Heard of It." Published January 14, 2019. https://www.weforum.org/agenda/2019/01/this-is-the-worlds-biggest-mental-health-problem/.

2.) "Depression and Other Common Mental Disorders: Global Health Estimates." Report from the World Health Organization, Geneva, Switzerland, 2017. https://apps.who.int/iris/bitstream/handle/10665/254610/WHO-MSD-MER-2017.2-eng.pdf.

3.) Martin, Elizabeth I., Kerry J. Ressler, Elisabeth Binder, and Charles B. Nemeroff. "The Neurobiology of Anxiety Disorders: Brain Imaging, Genetics, and Psychoneuroendocrinology." *The Psychiatric Clinics of North America 32, no. 3* (2009): 549–575. https://doi.org/10.1016/j.psc.2009.05.004.

4.) Swenson, Rand S. *"Chapter 9 – Limbic System." In Review of Clinical and Functional Neuroscience. Hanover: Dartmouth Medical School*, 2006. dartmouth.edu/~rswenson/NeuroSci/chapter_9.html.

5.) Richter-Levin, Gal, and Irit Akirav. "Amygdala-Hippocampus Dynamic Interaction in Relation to Memory." *Molecular Neurobiology 22, no. 11* (2000): 11–20. https://doi.org/10.1385/MN:22:1-3:011.

6.) Harvard Health Publishing by Harvard Medical School. "Understanding the Stress Response." Last modified May 1, 2018. https://www.health.harvard.edu/staying-healthy/understanding-the-stress-response.

7.) Lanese, Nicoletta. LiveScience. "Fight or Flight: The Sympathetic Nervous System." Published May 9, 2019. https://www.livescience.com/65446-sympathetic-nervous-system.html.

8.) Bonnet, Louise, Alexandre Comte, Laurent Tatu, Jean-Louis Millot, Thierry Moulin, and Elisabeth Medeiros de Bustos. "The

Role of the Amygdala in the Perception of Positive Emotions: An 'Intensity Detector.'" *Frontiers in Behavioral Neuroscience* 9, no. 178 (July 2015). https://doi.org/10.3389/fnbeh.2015.00178.

9.) Gordan, Richard, Judith K. Gwathmey, and Lai-Hua Xie. "Autonomic and Endocrine Control of Cardiovascular Function." *World Journal of Cardiology* 7, no. 4 (April 2015): 204–214. https://doi.org/10.4330/wjc.v7.i4.204.

10.) Fuchs, Eberhard, and Gabrielle Flügge. "Adult Neuroplasticity: More Than 40 years of Research." *Neural Plasticity* (2014). https://doi.org/10.1155/2014/541870.

11.) Gillespie, Claire. Sciencing. "How Did Isaac Newton Discover the Laws of Motion?" Last modified April 29, 2018. https://sciencing.com/did-newton-discover-laws-motion-5349637.html.

12.) Wegner, Daniel M. *White Bears and Other Unwanted Thoughts: Suppression, Obsession, and the Psychology of Mental Control.* New York: Penguin Press, 1989.

Chapter 4: Another Shot of Adrenaline

1.) Lois, Jennifer. *Heroic Efforts: The Emotional Culture of Search and Rescue Volunteers.* New York University Press, 2003.

2.) Mosher, Dave. Business Insider. "Buzz Aldrin Walked on the Moon 50 Years Ago Today. Here's What the Astronaut Remembers Most About NASA's Apollo 11 Mission." Published July 20, 2019. https://www.businessinsider.com/astronaut-buzz-aldrin-apollo-explains-what-moon-landing-was-like-2019-7.

Chapter 5: Exposure Is Your Anxiety Bulldozer

1.) Martin, Elizabeth I., Kerry J. Ressler, Elisabeth Binder, and Charles B. Nemeroff. "The Neurobiology of Anxiety Disorders: Brain Imaging, Genetics, and Psychoneuroendocrinology." *The Psychiatric Clinics of North America* 32, no. 3 (2009): 549–575. https://doi.org/10.1016/j.psc.2009.05.004.

2.) Rauch, Scott L., Lisa M. Shin, and Christopher I. Wright. "Neuroimaging Studies of Amygdala Function in Anxiety Disorders." *Annals of the New York Academy of Sciences* 985, no.1 (2003): 389–410. https://doi.org/10.1111/j.1749-6632.2003.tb07096.x.

3.) Goossens, Liesbet, Stefan Sunaert, Ronald Peeters, Eric J. L. Griez, and Koen R. J. Schruers. "Amygdala Hyperfunction in Phobic Fear Normalizes After Exposure." *Biological Psychiatry* 62, no. 10 (2007): 1119–1125. https://doi.org/10.1016/j.biopsych.2007.04.024.

Chapter 6: Stop Believin'

1.) Anxiety and Depression Association of America. "About ADAA: Facts and Statistics." Accessed 2019. https://adaa.org/about-adaa/press-room/facts-statistics.

Chapter 7: The Panic Attack Comeback

1.) American Psychiatric Association. "Panic Attack Specifier." In *The Diagnostic and Statistical Manual of Mental Disorders*, 5th ed., 214 Arlington: American Psychiatric Association, 2013.

Chapter 8: Having a Phobia Is No Utopia

1.) Culbertson, Fredd. "The Phobia List." Accessed 2019. https://www.phobialist.com.

ABOUT THE AUTHOR

Craig April, PhD, is an internationally known anxiety treatment expert and founder of The April Center for Anxiety Attack Management – Los Angeles.

Dr. April has appeared as an expert on TV news, been quoted nationally in magazines and newspapers, served as a frequent international radio guest, been featured on filmed panels, and speaks at schools, universities, business organizations, and other associations on the nature of anxiety and fear.

Dr. April was also a featured psychologist on the A&E Television show *Obsessed* for its two-season run. *Obsessed* was a documentary series, much like *Intervention* in style, that revealed the struggles of those with anxiety disorders as they underwent Cognitive Behavioral Therapy (CBT). Dr. April treated the show's participants with CBT's scientifically proven anxiety treatment techniques.

"I am committed to helping people break free from anxiety symptoms so they may live the life they are meant to live—one filled with calm, confidence, and freedom," says Dr. April.

Fascinated by the nature of his own fears and the realization that we grow by strategically facing discomfort, Dr. April nurtured this interest as he entered graduate school in 1991. By the time he obtained his master's in 1994, his PhD in 1996, followed by his licensure as a psychologist in 1998, Dr. April had extensively treated patients with anxiety disorders in clinic, hospital, and university settings.

Based on his continued focus in private practice working with those struggling with OCD, panic disorder, phobias, social anxiety, and generalized anxiety, Dr. April established The April Center for Anxiety Attack Management – Los Angeles in 2006 to provide specialized and proven anxiety treatment. The April Center offers individual, group, and family therapy, with anxiety treatment plans uniquely designed to make long-term progress as quickly as possible.

To discover more, visit The April Center website at KickFear.com.

9 781642 502169